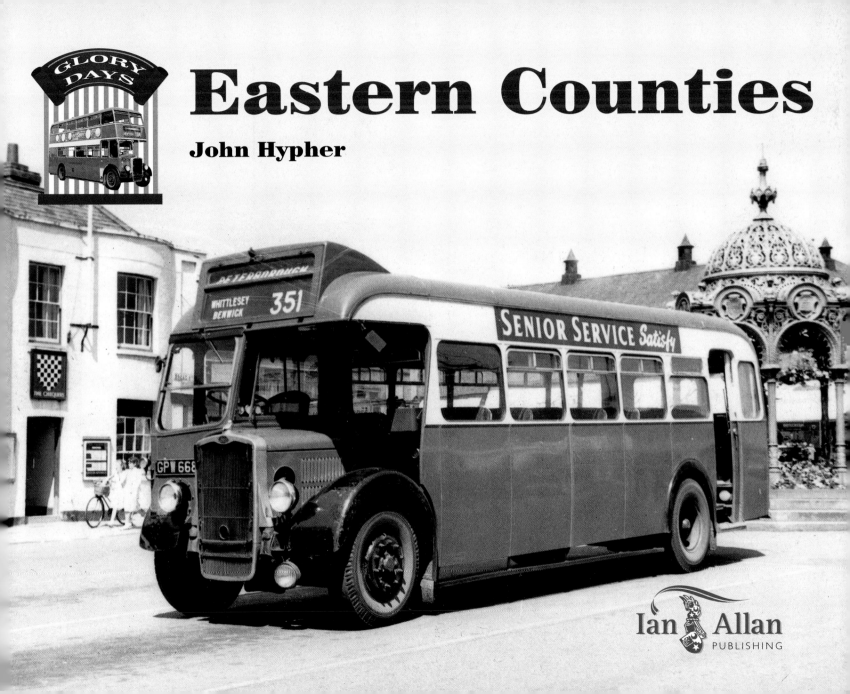

GLORY DAYS

Eastern Counties

John Hypher

Ian Allan
PUBLISHING

Front cover:
Bristol FS5G Lodekka LFS34 (2934 PW) picks up in Peterborough bus station before running out to Yaxley in August 1973. New in 1962, it would remain in service until 1978. Note the shorter radiator grille compared with LKD228 on page 49. *Malcolm Keeley*

Back cover:
Until the arrival of the Leyland National the Bristol RELL6G was the standard large-capacity single-decker. An early example, its 53-seat ECW body featuring a flat windscreen, was RL704 (TVF 704G), which entered service in May 1969. Seen in Cambridge during June 1972, it was to remain in service until 1984. *Mark Hughes*

Title page:
A 1948 Bristol L5G with 35-seat ECW bodywork, LL668 (GPW 668) is pictured in March before returning to Peterborough during June 1959. Of particular note is the rear door, which opens and closes on the inside (rather than the outside) of the body. This bus would remain in service until 1963. *Maurice Doggett*

Contents

First published 2005

ISBN (10) 0 7110 3069 3
ISBN (13) 978 0 7110 3069 5

Published by
Ian Allan Publishing

an imprint of
Ian Allan Publishing Ltd,
Hersham, Surrey KT12 4RG
Printed in England by
Ian Allan Printing Ltd,
Hersham, Surrey KT12 4RG

Code: 0509/x

Visit the Ian Allan Publishing website at
www.ianallanpublishing.com

Introduction

My personal recollections of the Eastern Counties Omnibus Co (ECOC) extend back to the 1950s and 1960s, from family holidays and extended visits to relatives, as well as trips taken to East Anglia specifically to check out the rich array of buses. The company covered a seemingly endless area embracing Cambridgeshire, Norfolk and Suffolk, as well as cross-county services into Lincolnshire and Essex. Having spent time in each of the counties, I developed a fair knowledge of the buses and services. Something of a soft spot grew for Eastern Counties, and it seems like only yesterday that Ls, Ks, SCs, MWs, PD1s and LDs were running through the cities, towns and villages. At the same time, Bristol LS, MW and Bedford SBO coaches, looking splendid in their cream and maroon livery, were provided for day-trippers and long-distance passengers.

There was also much to see on the municipal and independent front. Among a rich variety of buses and coaches in the area were Barton RTLs at Peterborough, Cravens-bodied RTs with Burwell & District, all-Leyland PD2s and Albion Nimbuses in Great Yarmouth and ECW-bodied AEC Regents in Lowestoft, while, until the summer of 1963, Ipswich trolleybuses provided the only instance of electric traction within Eastern Counties territory.

It came as a particular joy to join ECOC as a National Bus Company (NBC) senior-management trainee during the 1970s and to spend a happy couple of years with a company that already seemed familiar. Time was spent both at Head Office in Norwich and at most of the depots, many of which were old haunts revisited, but this time from the 'inside'. ECOC provided a mix of service types matched by only a handful of other NBC subsidiaries, operating express, excursion and private-hire coaches, intensive city services, radial country services to and from other urban areas, town services and a vast number of rural and market-day services. Depot sizes varied too, from the largest at Norwich (Surrey Street), through the other district centres at Ipswich, Cambridge and Peterborough, to smaller depots such as King's Lynn, March, Newmarket and Bury St Edmunds. Then there were numerous village outstations, ranging from one to half a dozen or so buses, which in many

ways represented the life-blood of many square miles of East Anglia. Digressing for a moment, outstationed buses were always kept immaculate by their crews and were significantly freer from mechanical failures than were their large-depot counterparts! Indeed, it was always a cause for concern when one of the outstationed buses was changed over for any reason, because it was feared that other drivers, particularly from the larger depots, would not treat the vehicle with appropriate care and respect!

The distance from Great Yarmouth to Peterborough is roughly the same as that from Norwich to London, which gives an idea of just how immense an area was covered by ECOC. In practical terms, the company was managed from Norwich, but in view of its size it was divided into eastern and western areas, based on Norwich and Cambridge respectively. This was further sub-divided into districts, namely Norwich and Ipswich in the eastern area and Cambridge and Peterborough in the western. These districts then had responsibility for a number of smaller depots and for the many outstations on their patch. It was a very logical structure, with a clear line of command, which had stood the test of time, with traffic and engineering functions being managed by their respective area, district or depot superintendents.

Historically the four districts can be traced back to the formation of the company in July 1931 from its four constituents, namely the Eastern Counties Road Car Co of Ipswich, the Ortona Motor Co of Cambridge, the Peterborough Electric Traction Co and the East Anglian section of United Automobile Services, based on Norwich. Later on the operations of the Norwich Electric Tramways passed to the new company, forming the basis of the city network.

In this book I shall present a picture of the Eastern Counties Omnibus Co and its predecessors up to the time of its privatisation at the end of its ownership by the National Bus Company.

John Hypher
Chelmsford
May 2005

◄◄ Seen in Cambridge in June 1963 on city service 101, Bristol KSW5G/ECW LKH311 (MAH 311) dated from February 1952 and would survive into NBC days, not being withdrawn until 1970. *Maurice Doggett*

1. Ringing the Changes

The world in which the Eastern Counties Omnibus Co had its earliest origins was a far cry from that of today. Suffolk, Norfolk and Cambridgeshire were very much rural counties, made up of many hundreds of small villages, hamlets and farmhouses. Indeed, the vast majority were farming communities which looked to their nearest market towns or cities for clothes, household goods, general merchandise and entertainment not available locally. Local farmers took their produce to market and if they had room on their carts would take some of their neighbours along as well.

At other times visits between villages or into town would have been made by horseback or by horse and trap. Carriers sprang up in many areas and transported goods and passengers by cart to a very slow timetable, with (for the human cargo, at least) no small measure of discomfort and exposure to the elements. By the early decades of the 1800s an impressive network of stagecoach and mail-coach routes had developed, and travel between London and the towns and cities of Suffolk, Norfolk and Cambridgeshire was readily available, if somewhat expensive! A selection of these were The Star, which ran between London and Cambridge, The Magnet, which travelled to Norwich via Newmarket, Thetford, Attleborough and Wymondham, and The Perseverance, which ran to Boston via Peterborough. Also available to the traveller was a pretty comprehensive network of cross-country stagecoaches, linking, for example Norwich with Lowestoft, King's Lynn with Wisbech, Cambridge with Northampton, Peterborough with St Ives and Great Yarmouth with Ipswich.

These coaches usually carried between 12 and 15 passengers, four travelling inside and between eight and 11 on the roof. But travel by coach wasn't as romantic as the pictures on Christmas cards would have you believe! Roads in general were uneven, muddy, stony, miry tracks which played havoc with both coaches and horses, not to mention causing extreme discomfort to passengers. Springing was very basic and nowhere near adequate to protect either vehicle or passenger. Passengers in those Christmas-card scenes would have had to endure not only jolts and lurching from the coach itself but

would also have been travelling without heat or any protection (if outside) in frosty sub-zero temperatures and possibly snow, biting winds or rain for hours or even days. Not surprisingly, perhaps, fatalities occurred due to exposure, passengers literally freezing to death or falling off the roof either through dozing off or being catapulted off due to the road surface! But these routes and enterprises — driven by the need for people to travel — were the forerunners of the bus and coach services operated by the Eastern Counties Omnibus Co and other such companies throughout Britain.

Things started to change from the 1830s, with the advent of the railways. Railway development throughout the country was progressing at fever pitch, with many lines being built simultaneously throughout the land. East Anglia was no exception, the first line opening between Great Yarmouth and Norwich in 1844. Within 10 years a significant proportion of the railway network in Suffolk, Norfolk and Cambridgeshire was in place, and by the turn of the century it had been completed. The plethora of railway companies which had promoted, built and operated these lines gradually reduced in number through takeover, amalgamation and consolidation, with the result that the Great Eastern Railway emerged as the principal operator in the region. With the statutory Grouping of the railways into the 'Big Four' in 1923, the London & North Eastern Railway (LNER) became the main rail operator in East Anglia.

A few years after the Grouping, in 1929, the LNER purchased a significant financial stake in the bus companies which eventually made up the Eastern Counties Omnibus Co, and it remained a major shareholder in ECOC until Nationalisation.

As the railways gained more and more of a foothold in terms of mileage and passengers carried, as well as speed, comfort and convenience of travel, they brought with them the swift demise of long-distance and, later, cross-country stagecoaches. Many of the carriers' carts disappeared too, for the same reasons, and with the later advent of local town- and village-based motor buses and trucks they trundled off into the pages of the history books.

2. Eastern Counties — the Family Tree

Peterborough Electric Traction Co

To the west of the region, Peterborough was (and remains) a focal point for many communities. A significant cathedral city and business centre, it was also the market town serving these communities. It was a fast growing city, much of its expansion being attributable to its developing brick-making industry, in which field it became a major player. Peterborough also enjoyed good rail communications, the first lines opening in 1845 and its link with London (completed in 1850) representing a significant landmark in terms of its future growth and development.

During the 1880s the first horse buses appeared on the city's streets but remained few in number until 1896, when the Peterborough Omnibus Co started running a small group of services from Long Causeway to Werrington, New England, Woodston, Fletton, Stanground, Farcet and Longthorpe. In 1879 several horse tramways were proposed, but for various reasons these schemes came to nothing.

By the end of the 19th century the British Electric Traction Co (BET) wished to operate electric trams in Peterborough but, having discovered the disadvantages to operators of the 1870 Tramways Act, boxed clever and instead applied for a Light Railway Order under the terms of the Light Railways Act of 1896. This was possible because the company planned to run its tramway outside the city boundary to Woodston and within the Soke of Peterborough as well as in the city itself. This did not require the backing of the local authority, nor was there the threat of compulsory purchase at a later date. The Peterborough & District Light Railway Order 1900 was granted, and construction work on the 3ft 6in-gauge tramway began in May 1902. The proposed line to Woodston was never built, but the three which were laid ran from Long Causeway to Walton, to Dogsthorpe and to Newark. The line to Walton was opened on 24 January 1903, that to Dogsthorpe opening a week later. Newark, however, had to wait until the end of March for its new tram service.

Twelve open-top double-deck Brush cars, each seating 48 passengers, maintained the service and were housed and

serviced at a new depot in Lincoln Road. They were joined in 1904 by a pair of trams which had seen service in Worcester and arrived in that undertaking's green livery, providing a sharp contrast with Peterborough's own colours of lake brown and cream.

BET's new tramway was operated as the Peterborough Electric Traction Co Ltd (PET), incorporated in August 1902, and remained as such until absorbed into the new Eastern Counties Omnibus Co Ltd. Motor buses carried 'Peterborough Traction Co Ltd' on their sides.

Surprisingly perhaps, PET never extended its tramway, preferring instead to use a small fleet of motor buses, in a livery of red and white, to extend its services and meet new growth in the city. In 1913 new services were introduced to Whittlesey, Crowland and the Deepings, but as elsewhere, further

▲ The driver and a very young conductor pose alongside their 1902 Brush tramcar, Peterborough Electric Tramways No 8. *Maurice Doggett collection*

A very short-lived member of the PET fleet, FL 536, a 1913 Straker-Squire with 26-seat Brush body, was requisitioned for the war effort and consequently saw little service with its original owner. Note the somewhat exposed seats both alongside and behind the driver. *Maurice Doggett collection*

held substantial shares in other companies. Both organisations had large investments in common in a number of companies and decided to consolidate and co-ordinate these. To achieve this, in 1928 BAT was renamed Tilling & BAT (TBAT), sometimes known as Tilling & British, with appropriate shares issued to Tilling. Outside this grouping both concerns retained separate holdings where one or other had sole interest. Thus in May 1928 PET came under TBAT control. However, no sooner had this been implemented than the London & North Eastern Railway and the London, Midland & Scottish Railway jointly purchased a 50% stake in PET under their entitlement within the Railways (Road Transport) Act of 1928. A new joint service (with Ortona) to Cambridge started in May 1928, and the route network was further extended through acquisition to King's Lynn and Downham Market.

Further vehicles operated during the latter years of the 1920s included Chevrolets, more SOS saloons and, from 1928, the first of a fleet of 14 closed-top Leyland TD1 double-deckers. In addition some Reos, a Lancia and some former London General B-type saloons joined the fleet via acquired operators. During 1930 the last of the new TD1s arrived together with some open-top Leylands from Ortona and a Dennis saloon from the Eastern Counties Road Car Co.

▲ development was suspended during the Great War. After the cessation of hostilities a new service to Woodston was started in 1919, to be followed during the early 1920s by services to Yaxley, Spalding, Grange Road, Bourne, Wansford, Oundle and Sawtry.

The earliest PET vehicles comprised Straker-Squire saloons and charabancs, which were followed by a quantity of Leyland, Garford, and SOS saloons together with some open-top Leyland double-deckers.

From the mid 1920s further new services were introduced, some through the acquisition of a number of other operators, including routes to March, Wisbech and Thrapston. Local networks based on Ramsey, March and Wisbech served the towns and villages in their respective areas.

In 1928 came a change of ownership and direction for the company. The British Automobile Traction Co (BAT) was a subsidiary of BET and had been set up to invest in the growing number of motor-bus companies. Another major player, Thomas Tilling, operated his own bus companies and, like BAT, also

By 1930 a selection of day trips was being run from Peterborough, including seaside trips to Hunstanton and Skegness. An 'Anywhere' ticket was also available for travel on all PET's services for just two shillings (10p!) on the day of issue.

During 1930 PET decided to replace its trams with buses, this taking effect from 4 August. To satisfy legal requirements while the paperwork was being processed a single 'ghost tram' ran on each route in turn until the necessary authority had been granted from the Light Railway Commissioners. The final tram ran on 15 November 1930 and was driven by the same driver who had taken out the first car in 1903!

The end of the road for PET came in 1931. Among the portfolio of companies under the control of TBAT were PET, the Eastern Counties Road Car Co of Ipswich, Ortona of Cambridge and the East Anglian operations of United Automobile Services. It was decided to amalgamate these into one large company, and on 14 July 1931 the Eastern Counties Omnibus Co (ECOC) was born.

▲ Peterborough Electric Tramways S14 (FL 4756) was a 1925 SOS S-type with 32-seat Ransomes bodywork. Transferred to ECOC in 1931, retaining its fleet number, it is pictured at Whittlesey before returning to Peterborough. It remained in service until 1937. *Maurice Doggett collection*

◄ Delivered in 1930, Peterborough Electric Tramways T13 (FL 8905) was a Leyland TD1 with handsome Brush bodywork featuring an outside staircase. Note PET's practice of carrying route boards on the sides of its buses. In July 1931 this bus was renumbered A42 by ECOC and three years later became AH42. Given a new highbridge ECW body and a Gardner 5LW oil engine in 1938, it received new chassis frames in 1945; the following year it had its body rebuilt by ECW and was renumbered AH342. Renumbered again in 1952 as AH755, it was withdrawn in 1953 and converted into a tree lopper (X33), surviving as such until June 1961. *Maurice Doggett collection*

Transferred to the new company were depots and offices in Peterborough, March, Whittlesey, Wisbech and Oundle, together with outstations at Chatteris, Ramsey and St Johns Fen End. Former PET services were renumbered into a new 3xx series. Also transferred to ECOC were 77 buses — 22 double-deck and 55 single-deck — of Dennis, Lancia, Leyland, Reo and SOS manufacture.

The Ortona Motor Co

The fine and historic city of Cambridge has a long and rich history. Oxford and Cambridge have vied over many years to be regarded as the world's foremost seat of learning, and you the reader, will have your own thoughts on the matter. Cambridge gained its rail link with London in 1845 and thereafter enjoyed good communications with its surrounding counties, and indeed, with the rest of the country. Its station, however, was located about a mile from the town centre, and it was this situation which encouraged the development of early public transport in Cambridge.

Cambridge Street Tramways (CST), a 4ft-gauge horse tramway, commenced operations on 28 October 1880. Its main route ran from the railway station to the post office, while a line from the CST depot in East Road joined the main line at Hyde Park Corner, and a branch line from this junction ran to Market Hill and later to the market itself. The initial fleet comprised six red-and-cream tramcars, each hauled by a single horse, which were later joined by a further pair of cars.

CST faced competition from the newly formed Cambridge Omnibus Co (COC) from April 1896 and ran its own retaliatory services until 1900, when competition ceased and each company agreed to keep to its own routes. A couple of years later, however, COC ceased operating. Further competition hit CST in 1905, when the Cambridge Light Blues Co and, shortly afterwards, the Cambridge Motor Omnibus Co (CMOC) appeared on the scene. Both were short-lived, and in 1906 CST was once again left in peace. However, the following year saw the remains of the CMOC rise phoenix-like from the ashes, when Mr J. B. Walford bought the assets of the company and started trading as the Ortona Motor Co.

A number of explanations, all with a nautical flavour, have been propounded as to how James Walford chose the name

'Ortona', one being that during a cruise in the Adriatic his boat docked in the small Italian port of Ortona, another that this was the name of another boat espied on the same cruise. However, a piece in the Cambridge Daily News in 1954 suggested that he simply went through a list of steamship names and picked the name at random.

Ortona started running on 19 August 1907 from the railway station to the post office and extended the route to Chesterton the following year. Green Ortona buses soon became a familiar sight in Cambridge and within a couple of years were running a local service from Mill Road to Oxford Road and other routes out to Sawston and Cottenham. Further new services to start before the advent of World War 1 ran between Cherry Hinton and Newmarket Road, while country services went to Willingham and Royston.

Meanwhile, during 1913, BAT became a major shareholder in Ortona and thereafter played a significant role in the company's direction. CST's financial position had reached an all time low and due to outstanding debts owed to Cambridge Corporation, the latter issued a compulsory winding-up order culminating in the closure of the horse tramway on 18 February 1914.

Ortona's early fleet was made up of Scott-Stirlings, Maudslays, Commers and Straker-Squires, most being double-deckers. As elsewhere, all development ceased during the war, but the 1920 timetable reveals new routes to Ely, Great Wilbraham, Burwell, Saffron Walden and Haverhill. Also included were afternoon and evening circular tours to such places as Newmarket, Royston, St Ives and Lincoln and whole-day trips to Felixstowe, Clacton, Southend, Great Yarmouth, Hunstanton and London; the coastal destinations were later served by regular daily summer services. From 1924 services were introduced from Haverhill to Saffron Walden, Thaxted, Steeple Bumpstead and Kedlington, further routes being added later in the decade. A route from Cambridge to Newmarket, together with a network of services based on Newmarket and running to Ely, Burwell and villages in the area was acquired in 1925, and the same year saw a new depot being built at Newmarket. Services in the Ely area were also acquired, and a new depot built in the town a couple of years later.

Following the war, more buses joined the fleet which included vehicles from Straker-Squire, Austin, McCurd, AEC,

A Leyland TD1 with 52-seat Brush body, Ortona 92 (VE 4208) was delivered during September 1930. Transferred to ECOC in July the following year, gaining an 'A' prefix to its number, it was later reclassified 'AH' to denote its highbridge body. A new, fully enclosed highbridge ECW body was fitted during 1938, and a Gardner 5LW oil engine in 1939. Following the war, in 1946, the bus received new chassis frames and was renumbered AH292. Renumbered again as AH746 in 1950, it was withdrawn in 1951. *Maurice Doggett collection*

Ortona 2 (ER 8804), an all-Leyland TD1 with lowbridge open-staircase body, joined that fleet in April 1928 and was numbered A2 upon transfer to ECOC in 1931. During 1937 this bus received a new highbridge ECOC body and a Gardner 5LW oil engine, being renumbered AH2. It was renumbered again as AH302 in 1946, in which year it was fitted with new chassis frames. Yet another new number, AH752, was carried from 1951, the bus finally being withdrawn the following year. *Southdown Enthusiasts' Club collection*

Leyland and Vulcan, again many bodied as double-deckers. The latter half of the 1920s saw the introduction of new Cambridge local services and country routes to Soham, St Ives and Bedford (joint with National) as well as expansion to services from Ely and Newmarket to further destinations. By 1928 Ortona had 85 parcels agents spread far and wide and a number of outstations. Excursions and tours continued to be operated, albeit with new Leyland Lion coaches in place of the older charabancs. As the decade progressed Ortona standardised on Leyland GH7 double-deckers until, in 1928, the new Leyland Titan TD1 with enclosed upper deck was adopted. Single-deckers, however, remained a mixed bag, with Dennis, Ford, Leyland, Reo, SOS and Star vehicles joining the fleet.

Ortona became a TBAT company in 1928, and the following year 50% of the company was purchased jointly by the LNER and LMS railways under the terms of 1928 Act described previously.

On 29 September 1931 the company was officially absorbed into the new Eastern Counties Omnibus Co. Existing service numbers were prefixed by a '1', which placed them into a new series allocated for Cambridge-area services. Some 93 buses (43 double-deckers and 50 single-deckers) and four coaches — mainly Leylands but also including Dennis, Reo, Star and SOS vehicles — and a Chevrolet lorry were transferred to ECOC. Premises in Cambridge, Newmarket, Ely, Chatteris, Cottenham, Haverhill and St Ives were signed over at the same time.

United Automobile Services

It may come as a surprise to some that United Automobile Services started life as a small and (for a while, at least) rather insignificant operator in Lowestoft, on the Suffolk coast. United was registered in April 1912, and its first route, from Lowestoft to Southwold, started in July. But the board had set its sights further afield, and three months later the company opened a new base in Bishop Auckland, Co Durham, from where it ran its first service in the North East to Durham. (The development of United's services in that part of the country are not covered further in this volume, which confines itself to those in East Anglia.) Back in Lowestoft, in January 1913 United took over those services in the area operated by the Great Eastern Railway, which had run its own buses since July 1904.

Having started in 1912 with just a couple of Halley charabancs, United had built up a fleet of around 30 Commers and Daimlers by the outbreak of war in 1914. However, its fleet in East Anglia was requisitioned by the War Department (WD), so everything remained in limbo until hostilities ceased, and it was only from 1919 that United could proceed with developing its services.

The aftermath of war brought onto the market a bonanza of cheap new and almost-new vehicles as the WD and AEC released a seemingly endless supply of AEC Y-type chassis. Workshops were established c1919 in Laundry Lane, Lowestoft, to overhaul, modify and refurbish both existing and acquired chassis, and these premises also served as a bus garage. A purpose-built body works was also erected, being ready for production at the end of 1920. For the first few years United bodies were built almost exclusively for its own fleet, but from 1924 orders were taken from outside customers. Output at this time was virtually all single-deck, and the backbone of United's postwar fleet consisted mainly of company-bodied AEC Y and Daimler CB vehicles. However, a few Y-type chassis were fitted with second-hand ex-London General open-top double-deck bodies, and United also ran a few short-lived 'lorry buses' with wooden bench seats and tarpaulin roofs. Smaller buses, for rural routes and to compete with other operators, comprised 14-seat Whites and a few Model T Fords.

Following the enforced hiatus during wartime, East Anglian services recommenced in 1919, when the Southwold–Lowestoft–Great Yarmouth and the circular Lowestoft–Oulton Broad routes resumed operation, while new services were introduced from Lowestoft to Beccles, Norwich to Cromer, Mundesley to Sheringham via Cromer, Great Yarmouth to Potter Heigham, Great Yarmouth to Somerton,

UNITED
AUTOMOBILE SERVICES LTD.

HEAD OFFICE:
KILBURN HOUSE,
FULFORD ROAD,
YORK.

Dear Sir,   October 9th, 1931.

On the 16th instant your employment with this Company will terminate owing to the sale of the East Anglian Section of the undertaking to Eastern Counties Omnibus Company, Ltd.

That Company will, however, consider an application made for employment similar to that which you are performing for this Company, and an application form is enclosed which should be completed and sent to Eastern Counties Omnibus Company, Ltd., 20, Lower Clarence Road, Norwich, before 16th instant.

A copy of the Conditions of Service of that Company is also enclosed for your information.

Should no employment be possible with Eastern Counties Omnibus Company, Ltd., a week's pay in lieu of notice will be given.

Yours faithfully,

A. T. EVANS,
Secretary.

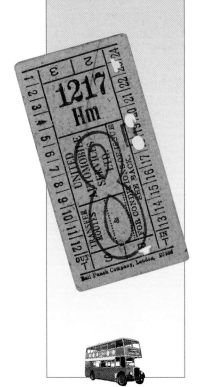

Norwich to Great Yarmouth and Norwich to Shipham. The early 1920s saw more new services, including a Norwich local from Thorpe to Foundry Bridge which was later extended to Catton Grove, as well as new routes from Norwich to Bungay, Costessey, Attleborough, Loddon, Beccles (ex Great Eastern Railway), Coltishall, Diss, Letheringsett, Holt, Long Stratton, Wymondham and Fakenham. Vehicles were based in newly acquired premises in Recorder Road, which also served as the Norwich terminus. United began running services at King's Lynn during 1920 but pulled out the following year, not returning until 1925, when it took over Norfolk Road Services and its services in the area.

Originally United buses ran anonymously in a grey livery with a blue waistband, but within a short time this was supplemented by the application of a blue skirt and United fleetnames. This livery was superseded from 1923 by a completely new look, vehicles being adorned with primrose below the waist and black above.

Bus services in all areas continued to grow and develop, new and revised routes being introduced and others joining the network through the acquistion of other operators. The Eastern District headquarters was moved from Lowestoft to Norwich during 1926, and the company head office relocated from Laundry Lane, Lowestoft, to York at the same time. Between

1926 and 1929 an associated company, W. T. Underwood, transferred to United some of its Lincolnshire services, including those from Boston to Spalding, Skegness and Lincoln, which joined United's own town and country services from Boston. A new service into Lincolnshire, from King's Lynn to Grantham via Spalding and Bourne, started in 1930, and further services in the King's Lynn area were added to the network through acquisition.

As well as running bus services centred on Norwich, Great Yarmouth, Lowestoft, Southwold and Cromer, United started to run express coaches to London, from Great Yarmouth in 1924 and from Norwich via Ipswich in 1928, the latter being extended to Cromer and Sheringham during the summer months. During 1928 United took delivery of some luxurious 20-seat ADC 423 coaches for its express services, many equipped with toilets and a buffet enabling refreshments to be served *en route*; they also had heaters and curtains and carried 'BUFFET CAR' lettering on their sides. By 1930 London was also served from Hunstanton via King's Lynn and Peterborough and by a further route from Norwich via Thetford. A number of cross-country express services were also operated, some jointly with other companies. Rival express operator Eastern Motorways of Norwich was taken over in October 1930, together with its fleet and services throughout East Anglia.

A fleet-renewal programme started in 1926, pneumatically tyred AEC 415s with single-deck United bodies being delivered in quantity. New vehicles continued to be steadily introduced until 1930, these comprising Chevrolet, ADC 425, Bristol B, Daimler CF (coaches), Leyland TD1 (double-deckers), Leyland TS3 (coaches) and Tilling-Stevens B10A2 types. Most carried United single-deck bodies, but the Leyland TD1s were bodied by Leyland itself, and the B10A2s by Short Bros.

The livery underwent yet another transformation in 1927, when it was changed to biscuit brown above the waist and yellow below, but this was destined to last only until 1930, when it was changed to red below the waist and white above. Interestingly, red would form the basis of both United's and ECOC's liveries for more than half a century.

A notable feature of the company's operations (which was to continue throughout the ECOC era) was an extensive parcels service. Parcels were carried on every route, and dozens of

agents were appointed throughout the region; indeed, so popular ▲ was the service that the larger centres, such as Norwich, ran their own parcels vans too. From August 1929 red letter boxes were carried on the last journeys of the day from Horning, Palling, Acle, Old Catton, Hethersett, Costessey and Drayton to Norwich, and from September 1930 the scheme was extended to include certain buses on the Boston–Skegness service.

During the latter part of the 1920s and into the 1930s the coach factory was kept busy constructing bodywork not only for United but also for many outside customers. By the handover to ECOC in 1931 the factory had constructed around 1,500 bodies, virtually all of which were single-deck. However, in the same year double-deck bodies were built on AEC Regent chassis for the Lowestoft and Great Yarmouth municipal fleets, and thereafter double-deck production became a normal part of factory life.

United remained as an independent company until August 1929, when it was purchased jointly by the LNER and TBAT, the two having equal shareholdings. As a prelude to the

Dating from May 1919, United 58 (AH 0519) was an AEC YD with 32-seat rear-entrance Liversedge body. It is pictured at Cromer with an unidentified group posing for the camera. *Maurice Doggett collection*

New in 1930, United A65 (VF 8508) was an all-Leyland TD1 with lowbridge 48-seat bodywork. During 1937 this bus received a new lowbridge ECW body and was re-engined with a Gardner 5LW unit. Renumbered A265 during 1946, it was withdrawn from service four years later.
Maurice Doggett collection

amalgamation of United's Eastern District with three other companies to form ECOC the General Manager of the Eastern Counties Road Car Co, Joseph Worssam, was appointed General Manager Designate of the new company; based from June 1930 in the new ECOC head office in Norwich, he assumed transitional control of United's Eastern District traffic function in readiness for the full District transfer, which effectively took place on 17 October 1931.

All of United's services and depots in Lincolnshire passed to the Lincolnshire Road Car Co during January 1931, before the formation of ECOC, while in Norwich the Recorder Road premises had become totally inadequate as a bus station, and from the same month services operated instead from the forecourt of Thorpe station.

The fleet which passed to ECOC was made up of an interesting assortment of 225 buses and coaches, of AEC, ADC, Albion, Bristol, Daimler, Dodge, Gilford, Guy, Leyland, Star, Thornycroft and Tilling-Stevens manufacture; of these, 146 were single-deckers, 64 were coaches and 15 were Leyland

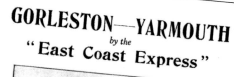

GORLESTON—YARMOUTH
by the "East Coast Express"

Luxurious Coaches
—
Refreshments Served on Board.

Hea duri
Cold We
—
Toilet
Accommod

DAILY SERVICES
From September 18th, 1929, until further notice.

			A a.m.	p.m 2.30
From LONDON	London (Bus Station, 1a, Lupus Street, Victoria)	dept.	9.0	
	Charing Cross (Gt. Scotland Yard)	pass abt.	9.8	
	Liverpool Street (Lyon's Restaurant, Tram Terminus)	"	9.15	
	397, Bethnal Green Road			Via Hendon and Norwich.
	Stratford (J. R. Roberts, The Broadway)	"	9.25	
	Manor Park (645, Romford Road)	"	9.40	
	Romford (30, High Street)	"	9.55	
	Brentwood (Yorkshire Grey)	"	10.10	
		"	10.30	
To LONDON	Yarmouth (United Kiosk, Hall Quay)	dept.	9.0	noon 12.0
	Gorleston (Hayman's Garage)	pass abt.	9.7	
	Hopton (Post Office)			Via Norwich and Newmarket.
	Lowestoft (United Corner)	"	9.15	
	Kessingland (Mr. Brock, Grocer)	"	9.30	
	Wrentham (Mr. R. Lansdell, Grocer)	"	9.40	
	Southwold (37, High Street)	"	9.50	
		"	10.5	

A Travel via Chelmsford, Colchester and Ipswich.

❖ Sundays Excepted

——— FARES. ———

	Yarmouth, Gorleston, Hopton		Lowestoft		Kessingland		Wrentham		Southwold	
	S.	R.	S.	R.	S.	R.	S.	R.	S.	R.
London	11/-	18/-	11/-	18/-	11/-	18/-	10/-	17/6	9/-	17/-
Romford	11/-	18/-	11/-	18/-	11/-	18/-	10/-	17/6	9/-	17/-
Brentwood	11/-	17/6	11/-	17/6	11/-	17/-	10/-	16/6	9/-	16/6

SEE REVERSE FOR FULL LIST OF BOOKING AGENTS.

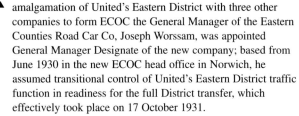

TD1 double-deckers. Other assets transferred included premises in Great Yarmouth, Lowestoft, Southwold, Norwich, East Dereham, Cromer and King's Lynn. Service numbers remained largely the same as those used by United, the block of numbers allocated to Norwich-area services being 1-99.

The Eastern Counties Road Car Co

Ipswich joined the rail network from London in 1846 and enjoyed good links with the surrounding area as well as the rest of the country. The town developed a healthy industry in agricultural implements, supplies, vehicles and machinery and also possessed a thriving dockland. Public transport was provided from 1880 by horse trams run by the Ipswich Tramways Co, but in 1901 Ipswich Corporation purchased the company and within two years had electrified the 3ft 6in-gauge system, which it later expanded. Horse buses, run by the Ipswich Omnibus Co, also provided services in the town for a brief period between 1899 and 1903.

The origins of the Eastern Counties Road Car Co (ECRC) began when brothers Walter and Thomas Wolsey went to Ipswich to investigate the viability of running bus services to the surrounding area. They borrowed four buses from Thomas Tilling Ltd for a trial period starting in June 1919. The experiment deemed a success, ECRC was registered in August, Thomas Wolsey and Thomas Tilling's son Reginald being among those joining the board. However, although the Tilling family made a significant early contribution to the company,

it was BAT which went on to take up the reins in terms of backing and management.

The initial fleet of 12 Tilling-Stevens TS3 double-deckers was purchased second-hand from Tilling, later being joined by 28 new TS3s comprising a mix of charabancs and single-deckers. However, by 1927 more than half of these had been rebodied as double-deckers.

Initial routes radiated from Ipswich to Felixstowe, Shotley Pier, Melton and Diss, soon being joined by others to Saxmundham, Stowmarket, Hadleigh, Debenham, Colchester, East Bergholt and Orford. A couple of services from Bury St Edmunds to Stowmarket and Diss were started in 1920, others soon being added to Mildenhall, Denston, Barrow, Sudbury and Walsham le Willows. Another area served by ECRC from 1920 was centred on Wisbech, an initial route to King's Lynn being followed by other services to places in the locality; however, these did not prove viable, and ECRC pulled out of Wisbech in September 1922. In contrast, the Ipswich area saw continuing growth with the introduction of a couple of town services and country routes to Walsham le Willows, Sudbury, Framlingham and Mistley.

◄ Posing for the camera before delivery in 1930, United AT80 (VF 7644) was a Leyland Tiger TS3 with a company-built coach body seating 29. The white board over the nearside mudguard was for route boards to be attached. During the war this coach would be painted grey, remaining thus until withdrawal in 1945. *Maurice Doggett collection*

▼ An unidentified Tilling-Stevens TS3 of Eastern Counties Road Car at Colchester in 1924. Note the combination of solid rear and pneumatic front tyres; also the large horn protruding from the front of the driver's cab. *E. G. P. Masterman / Omnibus Society collection*

As the network expanded further Tilling-Stevens buses joined the fleet. To give an idea of prices, 12 TS3A chassis delivered in 1925 cost £863 each, while their Tilling double-deck bodies were priced at £520 each. The Tilling-Stevens monopoly was broken the same year with the arrival of three small (14-seat) Morris buses purchased for £375 each.

The first Corporation trolleybuses started running in Ipswich from September 1923, and the following year ECRC offered to provide all passenger services within the borough. After considering the proposal, the Town Council rejected it, and the two operators continued to develop their respective services independently.

From the mid-1920s services continued to develop from the Bury St Edmunds, Stowmarket, Saxmundham and Felixstowe areas, and the 1925 timetable included charabanc trips from

Ipswich to a number of destinations, both coastal and inland. During this period ECRC acquired several neighbouring operators in its area, eliminating competition and adding new services to its network from Ipswich, Stowmarket and Felixstowe. 'Anywhere' tickets priced at 3s (15p) became available in 1928, initially on Mondays to Fridays only but later at weekends also, giving unlimited travel on all ECRC bus services. The same year a service was introduced between Southwold and Walpole, giving both United and ECRC not only a presence in the town but also separate depots in Station Road! A new Ipswich town circular service started the following year, centred on Valley Road and running effectively as two services travelling each way around the circle.

Between 1928 and 1930 a group of express services was introduced from Ipswich, linking the town with London (via

Colchester), with Norwich and with Great Yarmouth (both joint with United), with Cambridge (joint with Ortona) and with Clacton (joint with National), of which all but the last were extended to serve Felixstowe during the summer months; there was also a service from Southwold to London via Ipswich.

On the vehicle front, further Tilling-Stevens single-deckers and coaches joined the fleet, together with some small 14-seat Beans. Although Tilling-Stevens continued to be ECRC's preferred chassis supplier, other makes were purchased in small quantities, including Leyland Tiger TS2s, Dennis Gs and, in 1929, providing a sharp contrast with the incumbent open-top Tilling-Stevens double-deckers, the first enclosed all-Leyland Titan TD1s. Further TD1s purchased in 1930/1 came at a cost of £1,667 each.

In May 1928 ECRC became a TBAT company and from 1929 was owned jointly by the LNER and TBAT. Upon takeover by ECOC in July 1931 all services were renumbered into the 2xx series allocated to the Ipswich area, most retaining their original identity prefixed by a '2'.

▲ In January 1927 ECRC took delivery of this Tilling-Stevens B9A with 31-seat Tilling bodywork. No 37 (DX 6212) passed to ECOC (PA37) in July 1931. Rebodied in 1933 with a new ECOC 32-seat body, it survived to be renumbered PA917 in 1946, finally being withdrawn the following year.
W. Noel Jackson / A. B. Cross

Throughout ECRC's short existence all vehicles carried a red livery, with various degrees of white applied according to vehicle type. Along with four lorries, 127 buses and coaches — 76 single-deckers, 21 coaches and 30 double-deckers — were transferred to ECOC; the majority were Tilling-Stevens vehicles, but Chevrolet, Dennis, Guy and Leyland were also represented. Premises passing to ECOC included garages at Ipswich, Felixstowe, Southwold (this being retained in preference to the older United garage), Bury St Edmunds and Saxmundham, along with outstation buildings at Ardleigh, Barningham, Eye, Framlingham, Hadleigh, Sudbury, Walsham le Willows and Woodbridge.

Norwich Electric Tramways

Construction of the 3ft 6in-gauge Norwich Electric Tramway started in June 1898, and the system opened two years later, in July 1900. Rolling stock was made up entirely of maroon-and-white open-top Brush-bodied double-deck cars, of which 40 were built as motor cars and 10 as trailers. Norwich Electric Tramways (NET) operated from a purpose-built depot in Silver Road, this consisting of two car sheds which also included maintenance facilities; NET also built a dedicated power station, in Duke Street, to provide current for the cars.

During 1900 lines were opened throughout the city, these being centred on Orford Place, but before long severe

Norwich Electric Tramways car 29 heads along Earlham Road c1922. This 52-seat Brush-bodied car dating from 1900 would be rebodied by English Electric in 1927, thereafter continuing in service until the system closed in 1935. Pamlin Prints / Author's collection

congestion made this practice unworkable, and the following year the radial services were linked to form a series of cross-city routes. Colour coding was also introduced, the trams carrying coloured destination boards (and coloured lights for night use), enabling passengers to identify at a glance which route the tram was working.

From time to time the tram services were revised, and in 1914 statutory powers were obtained to run buses, to give NET a degree of flexibility in its service provision. The first of these ran in 1915 from Thorpe tram terminus to Thorpe Hospital, but this ceased at the end of hostilities, and it was not until 1925 that NET buses reappeared in the city in the form of Guy single-deck buses with United bodies. Placed in service when the line from Aylsham Road to the Royal Hotel was closed in April, they ran on two new services, from Duke Street to Mile Cross and from St Andrews Plain to Drayton Road. Later in the year two new tramway-feeder services were introduced from Earlham tram terminus, to Judges Walk and to Earlham, Five Ways. Further Guy buses and a couple of Bristols were purchased by the end of the 1920s, by which time the bus fleet stood at 19 vehicles, of which four were open-top double-deckers. Fleet livery for buses was brown and ivory.

Facilities for NET's buses were separate from those for the trams, and a new bus depot was built in Ladysmith Road, at the back of the tram sheds. In 1927 a new service was introduced from the city to the Heartsease public house, and further bus services commenced as more tram routes were discontinued. Between 1930 and 1933 a further 28 buses were purchased by NET. Twenty were double-deckers, of AEC, Bristol and Leyland manufacture, and the remainder Dennis and Bristol saloons. It is interesting to note that by this stage buses outnumbered the trams!

The story of the latter years of NET, culminating in its absorption into ECOC, continues in the next chapter.

New in December 1929, ECRC 140 (DX 8355), a lowbridge all-Leyland Titan TD1, passed to ECOC in July 1931, receiving an 'A' prefix to its fleet number, as seen here; note also the 'Bible'-type destination display. In 1937 this bus would receive a new highbridge ECW body together with a Gardner 5LW oil engine, becoming AH140. Withdrawn in 1948 and converted to a tree-lopper as X26, it would survive in the service fleet until 1959.
Maurice Doggett collection

▶ The new Eastern Counties Omnibus Co started out with a comprehensive network of bus services covering Norfolk, Suffolk and Cambridgeshire as well as express services under the day-to-day control of four district offices, at Norwich, Ipswich, Cambridge and Peterborough. Staff belonging to each of the four constituent companies received letters terminating their respective employments but in these were invited to reapply for employment with ECOC under a new and unified set of terms and conditions.

The new company inherited a fleet of more than 530 buses and coaches comprising a wide variety of chassis and body makes, vehicles ranging in size from 14-seaters to the new and impressive Leyland Titan double-deckers. Fleet numbers were allocated to all vehicles based on the United system, which included prefix letters to denote vehicle type. The first new buses to arrive with ECOC were 24 Leyland Titan double-deckers delivered in 1932, all of which carried lowbridge bodies; five were bodied by Leyland, the remainder receiving company bodies.

From its earliest days ECOC acquired significant numbers of small operators in its area. The takeovers provided new routes for the company, eliminated wasteful competition on others and produced something of a ragbag of vehicles, which in many cases were not retained for very long. The acquisitions continued apace until the early war years and would resume in the early 1950s.

A significant early acquisition was that of Bush & Twiddy (East Anglian Highways) of Norwich, in December 1932. Fifteen coaches, of AEC, Albion, Ford, Commer and Bedford manufacture, were included, but more important were the express services, which strengthened those run by the company and comprised routes from London to Norwich via Epping, Newmarket, Mildenhall and Thetford and a summer service from London to Great Yarmouth via Mildenhall and Wroxham. Further express-coach operators acquired the following year were Westminster Coaching Services of London and

Cambridge, Pullman Lounge Coaches of Great Yarmouth, Varsity Coaches of Cambridge and London and Varsity Express Motors, also of Cambridge and London. Westminster Coaching ran a London–Norwich service via Ware, Royston, Cambridge, Bury St Edmunds and Ixworth and a service to Bury St Edmunds via Baldock, Cambridge and Newmarket. Pullman Lounge ran from London to Great Yarmouth via Braintree, Sudbury, Bury St Edmunds, Diss and Lowestoft. As part of the Westminster deal, services between Cambridge and Hitchin, Cambridge and Bedford and Ipswich and Clacton were transferred to Eastern National with some coaches in November 1933. The Varsity companies ran two services from London to Cambridge, one via Bishops Stortford and the other via Royston; they also ran an Oxford service, which was transferred

to United Counties in April 1934 together with half a dozen coaches. With the elimination of competition and a greater choice of routes, together with a portfolio of new services acquired from these operators, rationalisation and a complete recasting of express services was implemented in January 1934; at the same time a handful of shorter routes were downgraded to stage services. The new network of express services, all of which continued to use the ECRC system of service letters, remained very much the same for many years.

Many of the acquired Dennis, Gilford, Leyland and AEC coaches were retained, some soon undergoing major surgery and a change of identity. The 10 Dennis F chassis from the Westminster fleet were converted to forward control (with the driver alongside the engine rather than behind it) and then

A Leyland Tiger TS4 with a company coach body seating 29, AT135 (NG 3879) was delivered new to ECOC in 1933. It is pictured working service T, operated between Liverpool and Lowestoft, jointly with North Western, the end-to-end journey time being some 14 hours. Note the outward-opening rear door. In 1943 this vehicle would be heavily rebuilt by ECW and fitted with perimeter seating. Renumbered AT935 in 1946, it was withdrawn in 1950.
Maurice Doggett collection

rebodied by the company with new rear-entrance 32-seat bodies during 1934. At the same time the six Leyland Tiger coaches from Varsity Coaches were stripped of their Dodson coachwork and fitted with new company highbridge double-deck bodies; five of these were allocated to Norwich Electric Tramways and the remaining vehicle to the ECOC fleet.

An interesting seasonal service, introduced in 1932, was a steamer-replacement service between Felixstowe Pier and Great Yarmouth via Southwold and Lowestoft, operated on behalf of the New Medway Steam Packet Co as an extension to the latter's London–Chatham–Southend–Clacton–Felixstowe steamship service! Allocated the service letter Z, it ran until the outbreak of war in 1939.

Further new vehicles were delivered during 1933, consisting of more Leyland Titans, this time TD2s with a mix of highbridge and lowbridge bodies, together with some Tilling-Stevens saloons and Leyland Tiger TS4 coaches.

Under the terms of the 1897 Norwich Tramways Act Norwich Corporation was empowered to effect compulsory purchase of the Norwich Electric Tramways undertaking after a period of 35 years. This meant that the Corporation had to decide in 1932 whether or not it was going to exercise its powers. The general feeling within the Corporation was that it should do so, but there was opposition from some of the ratepayers. A public meeting was held in December 1932 at which the purchase was rejected, and this was followed in

Dating from June 1933, Norwich 47 (VG 5545) was a Bristol GJW with highbridge Weymann body. It passed to ECOC as LG8 in December 1935, when the Norwich Omnibus Co was absorbed into the main fleet, and had a Gardner 5LW oil engine installed during 1938. Reclassified as HLG8 in 1950, the bus was withdrawn from service three years later. *Maurice Doggett collection*

A Bristol JJW with 32-seat coach body featuring a roof-mounted luggage rack, brand-new LJ4 (NG 9904) poses for the company camera in 1935. During the war its seating was arranged in perimeter style, but it reverted to normal seating in 1947, when its body was rebuilt by Cawood. Renumbered LJ434 in 1946, it was downgraded to bus duties during 1952, receiving red livery and roller-blind destination indicators, and survived a further four years, being withdrawn in 1956. *ECOC / Maurice Doggett collection*

January by a city-wide poll, in which the proposal to purchase NET was once again rejected, by a majority of more than 3,000. During October 1933, however, ECOC accepted an invitation from Norwich Electric Tramways to purchase a majority shareholding in the undertaking. This took effect from December, a board being constituted which included a member of Norwich Corporation. Thus Eastern Counties was now a tramway operator — albeit at arm's length — and had control of all NET's assets.

As noted previously, NET had already begun to replace its trams with motor buses, and it was agreed that the surviving trams be replaced at the earliest opportunity. During the 1930s more lines were axed, and in November 1934 ECOC promoted a Parliamentary Bill to abandon trams in favour of buses and to rename the NET undertaking as the Norwich Omnibus Co (NOC); at the same time future purchase options by the Corporation under the 1897 Act were removed. The Norwich Electric Tramways Act 1935 took effect from June 1935, from which date NOC buses were repainted into the ECOC fleet livery of red and cream, running 'on hire' to NOC, and

Wearing cream and red coach livery at Victoria Coach Station in September 1937 (and forming an interesting contrast with the Leyland Tiger behind) is LJ1 (NG 9901), the first Bristol JJW in the fleet. Built in 1935, it carries an ECOC 32-seat coach body. In 1938 it received a Gardner 5LW oil engine, and during the war its seating was arranged perimeter-style, this layout being retained until 1947, when it was rebuilt by Watson. Renumbered LJ431 in 1946, it was demoted to bus duties in 1952, being repainted red and received roller-blind destination indicators. During 1957 it reverted to its original fleet number and was withdrawn the same year.
G. H. F. Atkins / John Banks collection

renumbered into the main ECOC series. The last tram route, from Newmarket Road to Cavalry Barracks, ceased on 10 December 1935, following which the former NOC services were numbered 80-90, and ECOC services in the city (previously 7A/8/8A) 91-93.

Thirty new vehicles purchased during 1935 comprised 10 Bristol JJW coaches, 10 Bristol JNW saloons and 10 highbridge Leyland TD4 double-deckers, all with company bodywork; the TD4s were supplied with oil engines, heralding the adoption of diesel-engined vehicles as standard. The following year saw the delivery of 12 new highbridge double-deckers, consisting of a pair of short-lived Dennis Lances and 10 Bristol GO5Gs,

together with 10 Bristol JO5G coaches. Meanwhile, in December 1935, the Norwich Omnibus Co's 33 buses were formally absorbed into the ECOC fleet. (However, as a statutory company, the NOC could not be wound up without an Act of Parliament, and not until 1953 would the necessary application be made, Royal Assent being given in July of the following year.)

A very healthy order book was being maintained at the coach factory, the company's own requirements being fulfilled alongside increasing orders from many other TBAT-group members and from certain municipal operators. Interestingly, though, negotiations were in progress with Charles Roberts & Co with a view to selling the coach factory during 1933, but

DL1 (ANG 701) was the first of a pair of Dennis Lances with company-built highbridge bodies, delivered in 1936. However, after just four months the bodies were removed from these vehicles and the chassis returned to Dennis, where they were dismantled! The bodies — among the last to be supplied by the coach factory under the auspices of ECOC — reappeared on a pair of new Bristol GO5G chassis. *ECOC / Maurice Doggett collection*

The body fitted originally to ill-fated Dennis Lance DL2 appeared subsequently on new Bristol GO5G LG17 (AVF 359). Painted grey during the latter part of the war, this bus was rebuilt by ECW in 1944. Reclassified HLG in 1950, it is seen in later life in Great Yarmouth, displaying the vague kind of 'destination' for which ECOC was noted. Withdrawal came in 1955. *Maurice Doggett collection*

nothing came of this. By 1936 the factory was producing nine single deckers and one double-decker each week, with a staff of 950. In view of its size and success, the decision was taken to make it a stand-alone subsidiary (but still wholly owned) of ECOC, and from 1 July 1936 it became Eastern Coach Works Ltd (ECW). At the same time Laundry Lane was renamed Eastern Way — a name which was to become inextricably linked with ECW.

In January 1932 a new head office was opened at 79 Thorpe Road, Norwich, alongside the Cremorne Lane depot and workshops. Further major capital development was on the horizon in Norwich, culminating in the opening of the large depot and bus station in Surrey Street in March 1936. With the opening of these new premises Cremorne Lane ceased to be an operating depot, and the site was re-equipped and developed as the company's central workshops. Silver Road tram sheds closed after the final trams ran in December 1935, and Ladysmith Road depot was closed when Surrey Street became operational, albeit remaining in use for storage until eventually demolished to make way for residential development. The decade also saw new development elsewhere: municipally owned Bishops Road bus station in Peterborough came into use during August 1936, while Wellington Road depot and bus station in Great Yarmouth opened in 1937, replacing the existing facilities in Boundary Road.

In 1933 ECOC had embarked upon an extensive programme of re-engining, rebodying and overhauling its large and varied inherited fleet, this continuing until the early war years, when a scarcity of materials and manpower brought the programme to a temporary halt. Generally speaking, single-deck buses received Gardner 4LW oil engines, double-deckers and coaches being fitted with the more powerful 5LW. Thus 4LWs were installed in various ADC, Bristol B, Daimler CP, Tilling-Stevens and Leyland Tiger buses, while 5LWs were fitted to Leyland Titan TD1s and TD2s and as replacements for Leyland oil engines in TD4s, as well as to Bristol J and Leyland Tiger coaches. New ECOC/ECW rear-entrance saloon bodies, seating between 32 and 36, were fitted to ADC 415/416/423/425, Bristol B, Daimler CP, Leyland Lion PLSC3 and Tilling-Stevens B9 and B10A chassis, while a mix of new highbridge and lowbridge bodies were placed on Leyland Titan TD1s and TD2s.

In addition a pair of Tilling-Stevens B9Bs and half a dozen B10A2s were converted to forward control before receiving new company 36-seat bus bodies, the B9Bs undergoing further surgery during rebuilding through having their chassis frames replaced.

Meanwhile, further new vehicles were entering service. Bristol, itself a Tilling company, had by now become the principal chassis supplier to ECOC — as, indeed, it had to many other Tilling-managed TBAT-group members — while Eastern Coach Works continued to supply the company's bodywork requirements, and the entire vehicle intake for 1937 was of Bristol/ECW manufacture. Four were G-type highbridge double-deckers, six were four-cylinder Dennis-engined J-type

ECOC AH172 (DX 9024) on Norwich city service 91. A Leyland Titan TD1 new as ECRC 172 in 1930, it had its original lowbridge Leyland body replaced in 1938 by the ECW highbridge example shown here, having been fitted with a Gardner 5LW oil engine a year earlier. Given new chassis frames in 1946, it would eventually be withdrawn in 1952.
Maurice Doggett collection

Just three Fitt's vehicles — coach-bodied Dennis Lancets — were taken into ECOC stock, the remainder being discarded.

No new vehicles arrived during 1940, and 1941 was also a very quiet year, only seven saloons being purchased. Five were further bus-bodied Bristol Ls, these being joined by a couple more Dennis Aces out of an original order for five. Outside help came from Westcliff-on-Sea Motor Services in the shape of a trio of AEC Regent double-deckers, which remained on loan to ECOC until 1945. Things took a dramatic turn for the better in 1942, when some 40 Bristol Ls were delivered; both these and many of the 1939 batch ran during the war with perimeter seating for 31 passengers.

There were no arrivals during 1943, and just 16 new buses — all Bristol K-type double-deckers — joined the fleet over the next couple of years. Their engines and bodywork were non-standard as they came with six-cylinder AEC oil engines and bodywork by Park Royal (which provided six highbridge vehicles) or Strachans (10 lowbridge). The same period saw the purchase of additional double-deckers, in the form of a pair of second-hand Leyland Titans originating with Plymouth Corporation and a single AEC Regent from the Brighton, Hove & District fleet. (On a purely personal note, your author considers it a shame that ECOC never received any utility-bodied Guy Arabs, which rugged yet elegant vehicles epitomised the wartime double-decker!)

Soon after war had been declared in September 1939 there took place a mass evacuation of children from London to safer parts of the UK. Known as Operation 'Pied Piper', this entailed hundreds of train movements and the co-operation of local bus companies to move the children on to their destinations, ECOC supplying some 200 vehicles which transported children from around 30 stations.

With war looking more likely, and the supply of fuel likely to become a scarce commodity, Bristol Tramways had since 1937 been conducting experiments with producer gas, and as a result workable producer-gas units were available from 1940. One of the early units was sent to ECOC, where it was fitted into the rear of Norwich-based LN6, a Gardner-engined Bristol JNW saloon; this was followed by three further vehicles — Leyland Tiger TS4 AT136 at Norwich, Bristol JJW LJ2 at Cambridge and Bristol JNW LN7 at Ipswich. It was further

Dennis Ace D4 (CAH 924), with ECW 20-seat bodywork, was delivered in January 1938. Renumbered D974 in 1946, it was rebuilt the following year by Mumford but survived in this form only until 1949, when, along with its sisters, it was stripped of its engine, gearbox, axles and running units, which were destined for reuse in the chassisless ECW-Dennis buses delivered in 1950. *G. H. F. Atkins / John Banks collection*

▲ saloons, the balance being made up of 18 J-type coaches, six of which had six-cylinder AEC engines, the remainder Gardner 5LWs. Deliveries during 1938 were all saloons, 36 being the new Bristol L, of which a third were finished to dual-purpose standards. More small buses were needed to replace some of those inherited in 1931, and the Dennis Ace (or 'flying pig'!) was chosen to fill this role, the first eight of these 20-seaters arriving during 1938. A similar vehicle programme was adopted for 1939, which saw a further 10 Dennis Aces and a massive intake of no fewer than 50 Bristol Ls join the fleet; 10 of the Ls were dual-purpose vehicles, while a couple were bodied as full coaches, complete with curved-glass quarterlights.

In January 1938 Ely's network of services was boosted by the takeover of B. Washington of Littleport, while September 1939 saw the takeover of Fitt Bros of Norwich, together with a couple of city services, from All Saints Green to Lakenham and Tuckswood Inn, which it had operated for a number of years.

decided to convert one of the smaller depots to exclusively gas-producer operation, and from January 1942 Cromer's 11 Gardner-engined Bristol saloons — LN7 (by now transferred from Ipswich) and LL51-60 — ran on gas, all with trailers rather than self-contained vehicle-mounted units; those buses which had received the latter were converted. Ipswich, meanwhile, operated the only ECOC double-decker to run on gas, this being Leyland Titan TD1 No A146. More conversions took place during 1942, the vehicles involved being 11 petrol-engined AEC Regals (KA1-3, 5-10/8/9) which had previously been owned by Varsity Express or Bush & Twiddy.

Another bus to arrive with ECOC was Bristol L6GG LE1, which was already equipped for gas production. It was purchased from Bristol Tramways and carried its producer unit in the rear of the bus. It had a Gardner 6LW engine and measured 30ft in length — 3ft over the legal maximum. Because of the unusual circumstances of its construction, permission had been granted for its use. Delivered in July 1942, it joined the fleet at Cromer, after the war reverting to standard dimensions following removal of the producer-gas unit.

Despite a Government edict requiring 10% of fleets of 150 buses and over to be converted to gas, ECOC converted only the 26 buses described rather than the required 55. In the event this wasn't a problem; during September 1944 the Government announced a resumption in the use of normal fuels, whereupon all 26 producer-gas vehicles had their engines converted back to original condition, their trailer units being withdrawn, never to be used again.

Wartime brought with it other changes to the ECOC fleet and its operations. A new development, as elsewhere in the country, was the employment from 1940 of conductresses; needed to replace staff who had been called up for military service, they would remain a familiar sight on the company's buses until the early 1950s.

In order to conserve fuel and rubber many express services were suspended from September 1940, and this was followed by a daily curtailment of bus services from around mid-evening and also on Sunday mornings. For safety reasons some of the services around Felixstowe, Lowestoft, Great Yarmouth, Cromer, Sheringham, Mundesley and Hunstanton were suspended, while several services in other areas were also suspended to conserve resources. During 1940/1 nine ECOC vehicles — three ADC, two Dennis and four Tilling-Stevens saloons — went on short-term loan to London Transport. More than 50 of the older ADC, Tilling-Stevens and SOS vehicles were requisitioned and converted into ambulances, some of which did not return after the war; of those that did, many were put up for disposal as life-expired upon repatriation.

More than 200 single-deckers had their seating repositioned around the perimeter of the body, to accommodate many more standing passengers, regulations being relaxed to allow this. From 1942 around one quarter of the fleet was painted grey, to make them less conspicuous from the air; although a few double-deckers received this treatment, the majority were saloons. Headlights were also masked, greatly reducing the light emitted to the road and thus visible from the air; to aid visibility on the ground in Blackout conditions vehicles were given white tips to their front wings, together with a white line around the lower edges of the body and platform.

During the conflict ECOC vehicles and property were fortunate in suffering only relatively minor damage from air raids. The few buses which had been more seriously damaged were either rebuilt or rebodied, but none was bad enough to be written off. However, most areas of the company were affected to a greater or lesser degree, and perhaps the most destructive raid was a direct hit on Surrey Street at 6am on 30 July 1940; 16 buses were damaged, and the site was devastated. In order to avoid the possibility of large numbers of buses being destroyed or damaged during air raids, a proportion of vehicles were dispersed overnight from the depots to other parts of their towns and cities. In June 1940, as a result of a reduction in services and its vulnerability to attack, Felixstowe was temporarily downgraded from depot to outstation status, its fuel, oil and stores being transferred to Ipswich until after the war. The same month saw the company storing 45 Bristol chassis on behalf of ECW, which concern had (in May 1940, as a temporary measure) moved from Lowestoft to Irthlingborough, in Northamptonshire, because of fears of a coastal invasion; the chassis in question were held at Cremorne Lane (16), Silver Road (10), Ipswich (10) and various outstations.

During September 1942 ownership of Eastern Counties changed again when the Tilling & BAT partnership was

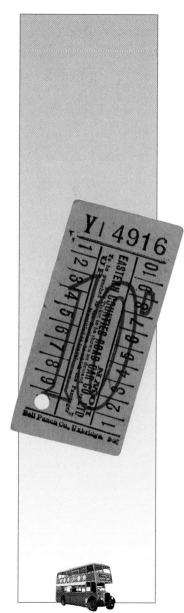

A Bristol L5G with an ECW body, LL96 (ENG 346) was delivered in April 1942 and ran during the war with perimeter seating before receiving conventional seating for 35 following the end of hostilities. Renumbered LL596 during 1946, it was fitted with the roller destination blinds shown in 1955. Seen working a Norwich city service in June 1957, it would be withdrawn later that year.
Maurice Doggett

dissolved; assets were shared between Tilling and BET, and ECOC passed into Tilling ownership. Hereafter its future would follow a path common to that of other companies within the group, which for a quarter of a century would be very different from that pursued by those which passed to BET. The war finally ended in May 1945, and a couple of months later Joseph Worssam resigned from his post as General Manager, to be replaced by C. H. Pickett, who would hold the reins until the end of 1954.

Although the refurbishment programme had been suspended, more than 100 vehicles were rebuilt by ECW, either to repair war damage or to make them fit enough to continue in service, although some of the more badly damaged vehicles, being too far gone to rebuild, received new bodies. Between 1944 and 1947 a huge rebuilding programme was spread among many other coachbuilders which included Mann Egerton, Marshall,

Mumford, Portsmouth Aviation, Beadle, Willowbrook, Abbott, Watson and Cawood, as well as the company's own workshops. The chassis of many of the early Leyland Titan TD1s and TD2s were getting rather tired — hardly surprising, given their age and service — so, to give them a new lease of life, between 1945 and 1947 some 70 of these vehicles had new chassis frames fitted, to keep them on the road until replacements were available. A small number of early Leyland Tiger chassis were similarly treated.

Apart from those services mentioned earlier and the acquisition of others from operators throughout the area, ECOC services generally remained unchanged during the period. In the eastern area around a dozen new routes were introduced within the Norwich District and a similar number in the Ipswich District, the latter including an Ipswich circular and half a dozen new routes at Bury St Edmunds. On the down side, the post boxes which had previously been available on a number of routes were discontinued postwar, thus ending an interesting feature of the company's operations. In the western area, the Cambridge District also introduced a dozen new services including three city routes. Peterborough saw just a handful of new routes (one of which would be run jointly with United Counties between Peterborough and Corby from 1947) but also service withdrawals at Oundle and from Stamford in Lincolnshire.

At the end of 1946 a new numbering system came into use whereby vehicles retained their prefix letters but were renumbered into a common series. Numbers 1-370 were allocated to double-deckers and 371-999 to single-deckers and coaches. Peacetime deliveries of new buses commenced earlier in the year with a dozen Bristol K double-deckers and half a dozen Bristol L saloons. A couple of the 'deckers had lowbridge Strachans bodies which were later replaced by ECW. Noteworthy was LK13, which had its upper-deck window surrounds painted cream instead of carrying the usual upper-deck cream band; this bus was also the first to be fitted from new with roller blinds (rather than the 'Bible'-style destination boards used hitherto); all future deliveries would be so fitted as standard. The following year saw a huge influx of 71 buses, comprising 40 Bristol Ls, 10 Bristol Ks, 20 Leyland PD1As and a Beadle-Dennis saloon. All the Leylands and a couple of the Ks had lowbridge bodies, and all vehicles save the Beadle-Dennis were bodied by ECW. However, 20 of the Ls were delivered with second-hand bodies dating back to

New in 1937, Bristol GO5G HLG21 (BNG 203) is seen in immaculate condition in Norwich during June 1957, its highbridge ECW body having been rebuilt by ECW during 1945 and the 'H' prefix to its original fleet number added in 1950. Despite its gleaming paintwork, withdrawal came later in the year. Note the typically helpful destination displays on this bus and the one behind! *Maurice Doggett*

New in 1947 as the fourth of four prototype chassisless vehicles to be built by Beadle, 33-seat Beadle-Dennis D999 (FNG 818) remained the sole example of its type to be purchased by the company. Powered by a Gardner 4LK oil engine, it lasted in service until 1959, being shown in the bus park at Peterborough bus station in September of that year. *Maurice Doggett*

Following the war a brief return was made to the Leyland Titan in the shape of 20 PD1A models with lowbridge ECW bodywork. Built in 1947, they remained in service until 1963/4. Seen in Great Yarmouth in August 1964, just before withdrawal, is AP351 (GPW 351). *John Hypher*

1936 (having previously adorned ADC 415s); these would be replaced late in 1951 by new ECW bodies. In 1948 there arrived a further 40 Bristol Ls and 26 highbridge Bristol Ks, which brought the total of much-needed postwar deliveries to a healthy 155.

Perhaps the most significant change of ownership to ECOC took place in 1948. The new Labour Government embarked upon a major programme of nationalisation, which included transport. Under the terms of the Transport Act of 1947 it set up the British Transport Commission (BTC), which assumed ownership of those shares purchased in bus companies by the railways following the 1928 Act. These included significant holdings in the companies owned by Tilling Motor Services, which decided to sell out voluntarily to the BTC; the sale actually took place in November 1948 but was backdated to the beginning of the year. Thus it was that ECOC and ECW passed into state ownership, the BTC owning the entire shareholding in each concern. At the same time the financial relationship between the two was severed, ECW becoming a separate BTC subsidiary in its own right.

Shortly to depart from Surrey Street bus station in Norwich for Halesworth is Leyland PD1A AP353 (GPW 353) with lowbridge ECW body. This bus started its service life in October 1947 and would remain in use until 1964.
R. L. Wilson / Online Transport Archive / Photobus

There were no obvious signs to reflect the fact that ECOC was now state-controlled, and things carried on very much as before, but as the years progressed it became increasingly similar to the other Tilling Group companies in terms of fleet composition, livery style, building design, staff uniforms, bus-stop flags and timetable presentation.

In the years 1948-50 the company received a further 260 new vehicles, bringing postwar purchases to more than 400. Most of these were of the usual Bristol/ECW combination, but some new types also came on the scene; joining the familiar Ls and Ks in 1949/50 were 16 petrol-engined chassisless Beadle-Bedford 35-seat saloons, together with 21 Bedford OBs with Duple bus (11) or 'Vista' coach bodywork. Beadle was also favoured with the order for three coach bodies, to be fitted to new Bristol Ls for delivery in 1949. However, many of the new Bristol/ECW double-deckers due that year would be unexpectedly delayed; London Transport was still suffering acute vehicle shortages following the effects of the war, and between January and May 1949 no fewer than 38 of ECOC's new highbridge Ks were sent on loan to the capital straight from ECW, the last not returning until June 1950.

In 1949/50 ECW rebodied 16 Leyland TD2s (13 highbridge and three lowbridge), and these received the deeper Coventry radiators to modernise their appearance.

In 1950 came further chassisless buses in the shape of 16 recycled Dennis Aces dating from 1938/9; their engines, gearboxes, axles and other units had been salvaged upon withdrawal, and their reincarnation was completed by the fitting of new 32-seat ECW bodies. These unusual vehicles remained in service for 11 years, all in the company's western area, before they were finally withdrawn.

At around this time Bristol's basic K and L models were modified to reflect new legislation that allowed more generous vehicle dimensions. From 1950 single-deckers could be built to a new maximum length of 30ft, and the consequential longer version of the L was designated LL. At the same time double-deckers could be lengthened by 1ft, to 27ft, the extended K type being known (somewhat perversely) as the KS. ECOC wasted no time in purchasing these new types as they became available. In 1951 further concessions were made, whereby the maximum permitted width of both single- and double-deckers was increased by 6in, to 8ft. The widened and lengthened K type became the KSW, the equivalent L type being the LWL.

One of the Bedford OB coaches with 29-seat Duple 'Vista' bodies purchased by the company was BS949 (KAH 949). New in July 1949, it remained in the fleet until 1957. *Maurice Doggett collection*

One of the 1950 batch of Bedford OB buses was B945 (KAH 945), with 30-seat Duple bodywork. Seen at Cromer bus station, awaiting departure for Sheringham, it would have but a short stay with ECOC, being withdrawn during 1956. *Maurice Doggett collection*

An elegant Bristol L6B with 28-seat Beadle coachwork working a private hire for the English Bowling Association. New in June 1949, LS493 (GPW 493) remained on coaching duties until 1955, when it was painted red and relegated to bus work, upon which it served until 1960. The body was then removed and a new breakdown/tree-lopper body built in-house, the resultant vehicle, numbered X40, serving until 1973. *R. H. G. Simpson*

One of the highbridge Bristol K5Gs to start its working life with London Transport was LKH115 (HPW 115), which was sent to the capital in February 1949 and remained there until the following February. It is seen working route 10 in Gracechurch Street in September 1949, complete with London Transport roundel on its radiator. Renumbered LKH428 in 1965, this bus would serve with ECOC until 1969. *J. H. Aston*

Delivered in September 1949, Bristol K6B LK366 (KNG 366) was built with 'standee' windows on the nearside lower deck of its lowbridge ECW body and ran for a while in this revised livery before being repainted in standard colours. Despite remaining unique in the fleet, it was to survive until 1966. *ECW / Author's collection*

This Bristol K5G with ECW highbridge body started its service life with London Transport, covering for serious vehicle shortages in the capital, and its depicted thus on page 36 (opposite). However, LKH428 (HPW 115) — until 1965 numbered LKH115 — was very much at home on Cambridge service 133 by the time this photograph was taken in the latter days of its career with ECOC, which was to end in 1969. *Photobus*

Keeping busy on Norwich city services is LKH160 (KNG 160), a Bristol K5G with highbridge ECW body. New in February 1950, it provided 19 years of service before being retired. *Photobus*

Looking splendid in its maroon-and-cream coach livery is Bristol L5G LE703 (KNG 703) with 31-seat ECW coachwork. New in April 1950, it would be officially relegated to bus duties during 1958, nevertheless still seeing occasional coach use until withdrawal in 1964. *Photobus*

Among the first deliveries to the newly created ECOC, in 1932, was this Leyland Titan TD2, although it looked very different then; when new as A194 (NG 2729) it had a lowbridge ECOC body and short radiator. In 1937 it was fitted with a Gardner 5LW oil engine, and during 1943 ECW rebuilt its original body, but in 1949 it was rebodied by ECW as shown, having received the longer 'Coventry' radiator before its visit to the coachworks. Renumbered as A8 in 1957, it assumed its final identity of A397 in 1960, being seen as such in Great Yarmouth that July, a year before withdrawal. Note the non-standard destination display. *Maurice Doggett*

Another vehicle to undergo a major transformation was A212 (NG 5403), a Leyland TD2 new in 1933 with highbridge ECOC body. Renumbered AH212 in 1934, it received a Gardner 5LW oil engine in 1937 and was rebuilt by ECW in 1942, gaining a longer radiator and a new highbridge ECW body eight years later. In 1958 it was renumbered again as AH23, in which guise it is pictured in Surrey Street bus station, Norwich, in June 1959. Withdrawal would come the following year. *Maurice Doggett*

Unusual buses were 16 chassisless vehicles built by Eastern Coach Works during 1950 using engines, gearboxes and running units salvaged from withdrawn Dennis Aces dating from 1938/9. Numerically the last, CD847 (HPW 832) was photographed at King's Lynn in April 1960. *Maurice Doggett*

Another of the unusual ECW-Dennis rebuilds was CD844 (HPW 829), which would remain in service until 1961. Seating was provided for 32 passengers. *Photobus*

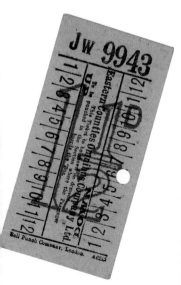

Built to the newly legalised maximum length of 30ft, LL725 (LNG 725), a Bristol LL5G with 39-seat ECW bodywork, was new in January 1951. It is pictured at Felixstowe in August 1965, two years before withdrawal.
Maurice Doggett

The first Bristol KS to join the ECOC fleet arrived in September 1950 in the shape of LK280 (LNG 280). Pictured at Felixstowe in August 1964, it would be withdrawn a couple of years later, in 1966.
Maurice Doggett

One of the Bristol LWL6Bs with 31-seat ECW coachwork, at London Victoria in October 1962. One of five such vehicles in the ECOC fleet with this new style of coachwork, LS705 (KNG 705) dated from May 1951 and would be withdrawn in 1966. *Maurice Doggett*

Showing its 30ft length to advantage is LL737 (LNG 737), allocated to Cambridge. A 1951 Bristol LWL5G with 39-seat ECW body, it was among the last rear-entrance, front-engined saloons to be purchased by ECOC and would serve the company until 1968. *Photobus*

During 1951 ECOC received examples of both these new types, five of its LWLs featuring ECW's curvaceous new full-fronted coach body; these heralded a new coach livery of cream with black wings.

A strange combination of narrow chassis and wide bodywork was applied to 11 KS 'deckers and seven LL saloons in 1951. Nos LKH261-5, LKII295-300 and LL729-35 were built with 8ft-wide bodies, which looked somewhat uncomfortable, mounted on 7ft 6in chassis! This mismatch would be perpetuated during 1953, when 18 earlier Ks received new 8ft bodies (12 lowbridge and six highbridge) courtesy of ECW; like the aforementioned Leyland TD2s these were also given PV2 radiators, for cosmetic reasons.

Perhaps the most significant vehicle of 1951 was the company's first example of the new underfloor-engined front-entrance Bristol LS saloon, developed jointly by Bristol and ECW. Numbered LL744, this, the second prototype, was delivered to ECOC as LL744 in July (and would remain in the fleet until 1972, when it was preserved by the company in view of its developmental significance).

The acquisition of rival operators recommenced during 1951, and, as in the past, the result in service terms was the elimination of wasteful competition, the acquisition of new routes and the incorporation of others into revised ECOC services. Reynolds Garages, trading as Metropolitan Coaches, of Great Yarmouth was acquired in July. However, in contrast with all previous acquisitions, the vehicles (including subsequent new deliveries of Bristol and Bedford coaches based at Great Yarmouth) retained Metropolitan Coaches fleetnames until the end of the 1967 season. July 1951 also saw the arrival of a pair of Gurney Nutting-bodied Maudslay Marathon coaches consequent upon the takeover of B. Beeston & Son of East Bergholt. Given that it had achieved a fair degree of vehicle standardisation, it was surprising that the company should retain the varied array of non-standard types which came with the various operators it had acquired. During 1951 such vehicles included Commer, Dennis, Leyland, Albion, Maudslay, Austin, AEC and Bedford models.

Between 1951 and 1955 a transition was taking place between the old order and the new, and a new benchmark in vehicle design began to emerge. The last rear-entrance, half-cab, front-engined L-type saloons had been delivered in 1951, and the following year's intake consisted of five production examples of the Bristol LS front-entrance, underfloor-engined saloon, which was suitable for one-man operation (OMO) and offered a higher seating capacity. Some 16 modern and airy LS coaches and dual-purpose vehicles also joined the fleet, as did 18 Bedford SBOs with Duple coachwork; these latter were the only examples of their type to be built with the Gardner 4LK engine in lieu of the more usual Perkins unit. Of the LS vehicles, most of the coaches were supplied with five-cylinder engines, while some of the buses had to make do with just four cylinders — in each case one cylinder fewer than was the case with deliveries to most other fleets.

Seen working the Cherry
Hinton service 131 in
Cambridge is Bristol K5G
LKH247 (FNG 145). Its ECW
body, new in 1953 (and, at 8ft,
6in wider than the chassis),
replaced the lowbridge
Strachans body with which the
vehicle was delivered in
November 1945. The bus
would be taken out of service
in 1969. *Photobus*

Delivered in July 1951, LL744
(MAH 744) was the second
prototype of the underfloor-
engined Bristol/ECW LS
design and was powered by a
four-cylinder Gardner engine.
Seen in its original livery on
Ipswich circular service 239,
it would clock up 21 years'
service before being retired and
preserved by the company.
Maurice Doggett

Pictured at Norwich's Surrey Street bus station in standard bus livery is LL744 (MAH 744), with 42-seat ECW bodywork. This bus was the second prototype Bristol LS bus and entered service in July 1951. Because of its importance as a major landmark in bus development it was kept by ECOC as a preserved vehicle after its withdrawal in 1972. It is currently on long-term loan to the Eastern Transport Collection Society and can still be seen at bus rallies during the summer season. *Photobus*

Over the years, as a result of taking over smaller operators, ECOC acquired vehicles of all shapes and sizes. A Maudslay Marathon III with 37-seat Gurney Nutting coachwork, MS908 (LRT 134) was one of a pair ordered by B. Beeston & Son of East Bergholt but delivered direct to ECOC in June 1951, one month before that concern was formally taken over. Pictured in Ipswich, it enjoyed 11 years of service before being withdrawn in 1962. *R. H. G. Simpson*

Highbridge Bristol KSW5G LKH318 (MAH 318) approaches the top end of Surrey Street bus station. New in March 1952, this bus would give 19 years of service, taking it into the early years of NBC ownership. *Photobus*

Seen in its attractive dual-purpose livery, Bristol LS4G LE749 (MAH 749), with 39-seat ECW bodywork, entered service in May 1953 and was fitted for OMO during 1962. Having lost its semi-coach seats in 1968, it would be taken out of service three years later. *R. L. Wilson / Online Transport Archive / Photobus*

On the early LS coaches the cream paintwork was relieved by red or black window surrounds and black wings, until the company decided upon maroon for these features, while from the mid-1950s the upper-case block-style gold 'EASTERN COUNTIES' fleetname already carried by the coaches was extended to the bus fleet. The new coach fleet also brought the company some new-found prestige, ultimately bringing two consecutive wins at the British Coach Rally; at the inaugural event, held at Clacton in 1955, LS765 took second place in the Concours d'Elégance, and the following year, at Brighton, LS766 went one better, winning the Concours outright!

Another unusual and unique vehicle to join the fleet (following the lone Beadle-Dennis of 1947) was N973, an Albion FT39L ordered by Beeston's but delivered direct to ECOC following the takeover. Fitted with a specially built ECW body, the bus entered service in June 1953 and would remain active until 1967.

Company workshops were being kept busy not only with routine maintenance and repairs but also with modifications, upgrades, downgrades and a host of other activities. In readiness for a new seasonal service at Felixstowe starting in 1952 a pair of former Norwich Omnibus Co Bristol GJWs (HLG4 and HLG6) were converted to open-top earlier in the year and painted cream with black wings.

In the quest to remove as many six-cylinder engines as possible from the fleet, many of the Bristol Ks dating from 1944-52 still running with these units would be changed between 1952 and 1961 with replacement Gardner 5LW units. Several Bristol J and L saloons were similarly treated, and in 1952/3 the Beadle-Bedfords lost their Bedford petrol engines in favour of Gardner 4LK diesel units to give them company-wide versatility, only certain depots being equipped with petrol pumps.

The year 1954 saw the introduction of the new low-height Bristol LD Lodekka, which was a joint development between Bristol and ECW. The Lodekka was built to lowbridge dimensions but to highbridge layout, with a central gangway upstairs rather than the hitherto obligatory offside sunken gangway to save on height; its low-height design also gave a step-free entrance from the platform to the lower saloon. The advantage of this design of bus was that it could operate on any double-deck route without concerns over height. Once more, a

new benchmark was being set in vehicle design. During 1954 four Lodekkas were purchased, a further seven joining them the following year, and these became the standard ECOC double-decker for the next 16 years. Again, these were not as most other Bristols elsewhere, as the tradition of specifying one cylinder fewer than normal was perpetuated, and these ran on five.

Yet another new type of bus joined the fleet during 1955, this being the new lightweight Bristol SC saloon, with forward-entrance, full-fronted ECW body; 27ft 6in long and 7ft 6in wide, this was designed for use on the kind of rural routes in which ECOC's territory abounded, the first to arrive with the company, in December 1955, being the third prototype.

One of the eccentricities of ECOC lay in its vehicle destination displays, which were known as the 'Bible' type, with destination boards laid out like verses. Although the last new buses equipped with these were delivered in 1946, displays of this style continued in use well into the following decade; it was finally decided to replace them on surviving saloons from 1955, and by the summer of 1957 they had vanished from sight.

▲ The 1954 Bedford SBOs with 37-seat Duple 'Vega' coachwork were powered by Gardner 4LK oil engines — a combination unique to ECOC — rather than the more usual Perkins units. Photographed approaching Victoria Coach Station, BV858 (PPW 858) would serve the company until 1966. *R. H. G. Simpson*

Delivered during 1953 was this unique Albion FT39L, N973 (NAH 973), with 35-seat ECW body. The Albion chassis had been ordered by B. Beeston & Son of East Bergholt prior to that firm's takeover by ECOC in July 1951, but the body was ordered separately by the company from ECW. In 1965 this bus was renumbered N999, in which guise it is seen in Ipswich bus station in June 1966. It would be withdrawn the following year. *Maurice Doggett*

Pictured at Felixstowe Dock while working the seasonal seafront service in September 1959 is HLG4 (VG 5541). A Weymann-bodied Bristol GJW, this bus started life in June 1933 as Norwich Electric Tramways 43, being renumbered LG4 when absorbed into the main ECOC fleet in December 1935 and fitted with a Gardner 5LW oil engine in 1938. The 'H' was added to its fleet number in 1950 to denote its highbridge body, and in 1952 it was converted to open-top. Renumbered again during 1960, as HLG496, it would be withdrawn at the end of that season. *Maurice Doggett*

◀ The second Bristol Lodekka to enter service with ECOC was LKD228 (OVF 228). New in July 1954, this Bristol LD5G with 58-seat ECW bodywork shows the long 'apron'-type grille which characterised the early examples of these vehicles and which would be superseded by the style shown on LFS34 on the front cover. Photographed while operating Ipswich town circular service 239, it would be withdrawn in 1971. *Photobus*

Of note also was the replacement on K types and some of the Ls of existing front roller-blind displays with side-by-side two-aperture destination and number displays. A number of Ks were also modified with 'T'-style displays at the front and/or rear in the mid-1960s.

From 1956 to 1959 deliveries of Bristol buses and coaches continued. These included 64 SC-type buses, of which one, LC565 of 1959, was one of two (the other being delivered to Crosville) notable in having a fibreglass body. It was instantly recognisable during its first few years in service through being painted all-over red, remaining as such until 1964, when it received the more usual cream relief around the windows. In 1956/7 a batch of 10 coach-seated SCs, finished in cream and maroon, joined the fleet; unlike the buses these lacked the small outline Bristol grille with side vents, most having merely an aperture with recessed black mesh, making them somewhat

bland in appearance, although the last three featured triple-horizontal grilles, as supplied elsewhere on rebodied Ls and SC coaches. During this period 44 new Lodekkas were delivered, powered, as before, by five-cylinder engines. Four LS buses and a dozen coaches entered service in 1956/7 and were the last vehicles of this type to be delivered to ECOC, being superseded from 1958 by the new Bristol MW. A revised body was designed by ECW for both bus and coach versions, and the company took 27 buses and 13 coaches in 1958/9. To give an idea of bus prices, in 1958 a Lodekka cost £5,000, an SC saloon £3,500, an MW saloon £4,750, and an MW coach £5,250.

Despite the significant intake of new vehicles, ECOC was still short of double-deckers and in 1959 acquired a pair of Bristol Ks from the West Yorkshire Road Car Co and a trio of similar buses from the Bristol Omnibus Co, most surviving until 1962.

A 1956 coach-seated Bristol SC4LK with 33-seat ECW body, LSC872 (TVF 872) approaches Victoria Coach Station in the early 1960s. One of 10 such vehicles, delivered in batches of seven and three, it was fitted for OMO in 1965 for its last two years of service.
R. H. G. Simpson

New in May 1957, Bristol LS5G LS773 (VVF 773) with 39-seat ECW coachwork epitomises the new generation of airy, underfloor-engined front-entrance coaches. Captured on film at Felixstowe in July 1965, it would shortly be modified for bus duties by the fitting of electrically operated jack-knife doors, bus-type destination indicators and OMO equipment. It would be painted into NBC dual-purpose livery in 1973 and withdrawn a couple of years later.
Maurice Doggett

From 1960 all Lodekkas were of the new flat-floor F-series version, which went into production the same year. By 1963 some 66 FS-type Lodekkas, powered by the usual five-cylinder engines (as, indeed, were all subsequent buses of this type), had entered service; of these, 25 featured offside illuminated advert panels which were backlit with fluorescent lighting. Another new feature, introduced on the 1963 Lodekkas (LFS65-9), was the Cave-Browne-Cave heating/ventilation system, whereby a conventional radiator was replaced by a pair of intake grilles (situated on either side of the front destination display) which provided cooling for the engine and heating for the bus. Perhaps surprisingly, apart from some FLFs acquired later, these remained the only company Lodekkas to feature CBC equipment. ECOC's first 30ft-long Lodekkas arrived in 1963 in the shape of six 70-seater FLs; these carried 10 more seats than their LD and FS counterparts and featured six-cylinder Bristol BVW engines. At the end of 1962 a pair of Bristol K convertible open-toppers were bought second-hand from Brighton, Hove & District to replace the ageing ex-Norwich Omnibus Bristol GJWs on the Felixstowe seafront service.

The final 13 SCs entered service during 1960/1, but MW saloons continued to be purchased, a further nine arriving in 1961, and 24 in 1963. In 1960/1, meanwhile, came a dozen more MW coaches, but in 1962 20 MW coaches of a totally new design gave an ultra-modern look to the coach fleet. ECW had designed a completely new body, which featured more curves and glass and created a fine coach which looked as if it had been specially designed for the purpose rather than being a modified bus shell with coach seats inside. The company wasted no time in exploiting the good looks of these vehicles in publicity for its private-hire and coaching activities.

In terms of vehicle development, the Tilling years saw great strides being made in both chassis and body design from an overall front-engined standard, to underfloor-engined buses and coaches, and then to the start of a new rear-engined standard which still remains with the industry today. In 1961 the regulations were again modified to allow the construction of single-deckers to a new maximum length of 36ft. Bristol and ECW had been developing a new generation of rear-engined saloons and coaches and the first of these to enter service with ECOC were three 47-seat RELH coaches in 1964. They were

the first 36ft-long vehicles in the fleet, and their body design was based on that of the MWs mentioned earlier. ECW's designers certainly knew what they were doing, as despite being rear-engined these vehicles still retained the traditional luggage boot. A further 15 similar coaches arrived during 1965/6. The RE family also included buses, the shorter version being the RESL, and the 36ft version the RELL. ECOC received 14 RESLs in 1967 followed by 20 RELLs during 1968. The days of the MW were now numbered, and final orders for the type saw 12 coaches delivered during 1964 and 45 buses between 1964 and 1966. Of particular note were two of the last MWs to join the fleet, late in 1966. Numbered LM640/1, they were built with dual entrance/exits and had 30 seats arranged to enable 30 standing passengers to be accommodated more comfortably. As built, LM640 had forward-facing seats, double on both sides to the centre door and single beyond, again on both sides, while LM641 had single seats on the offside and double on the nearside, again all forward-facing, along the full length of the saloon; both buses had five forward-facing seats against the rear bulkhead. Entering service in November, they ran thus for only a couple of weeks before being taken out of service, ultimately re-emerging as standard buses with centre exits removed and modified to the normal 45-seat layout.

A further 54 FS Lodekkas arrived during 1964/5, after which the type gave way to the 70-seat FLF forward-entrance version. Like the FLs these were 30ft long and came with six-cylinder engines. From 1966 to 1968 the company took 82 FLFs, some of which would have a short working life in East Anglia, as we shall see later.

After several years of exclusively Bristol orders ECOC turned once again to Bedford, four ECW-bodied VAM buses arriving during 1967, and 10 Duple-bodied VAM coaches in 1967/8. Meanwhile, a new lightweight Bristol model, known as the LH, was introduced. The company took eight of these in 1968, the last of the batch (LH692) being exhibited at the 1968 Commercial Motor Show.

A common practice among large operators was the downgrading of old coaches for bus work, to maximise their use before disposal. ECOC was no exception, and throughout the 1950s and '60s coaches ranging from prewar Bristol Js to

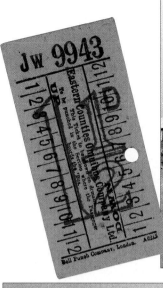

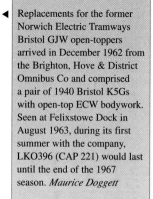

Replacements for the former Norwich Electric Tramways Bristol GJW open-toppers arrived in December 1962 from the Brighton, Hove & District Omnibus Co and comprised a pair of 1940 Bristol K5Gs with open-top ECW bodywork. Seen at Felixstowe Dock in August 1963, during its first summer with the company, LKO396 (CAP 221) would last until the end of the 1967 season. *Maurice Doggett*

Some 78 bus-bodied Bristol SC4LKs were operated by ECOC, this example being one of the last of the type to be purchased, in 1961. Seen in Peterborough bus station before setting out for Walton, LC576 (6576 NG), with 35-seat ECW body, would serve the company until 1972. *Photobus*

Pausing in the sunshine at King's Lynn while working a local service, LFS72 (72 DPW) shows very well its livery of Tilling red and cream with black lining-out. A 1963 Bristol Lodekka FS5G featuring the final style of radiator grille, it would remain in the fleet until 1981. *Malcolm Keeley*

53

Standard Bristol MW5G bus LM491 (491 DPW), with 45-seat ECW bodywork, enters Cromer bus station on service 22 bound for Overstrand. New in November 1963, this vehicle would be renumbered LM991 during 1965 and withdrawn in 1977. *R. L. Wilson / Online Transport Archive / Photobus*

In original coach form, LS801 (4827 VF), a 1961 Bristol MW6G with 39-seat ECW bodywork draws into Colchester bus station c1968. This vehicle would be relegated to bus duties and converted for OMO in 1970, being fitted (by ECW) with bus-type indicators in 1971; two years later it would be painted in NBC dual-purpose livery, surviving thus until 1977. *Photobus*

With its cream and maroon paintwork gleaming in the sunshine, LS805 (3805 PW) waits in Peterborough bus station before setting out for Felixstowe on service D. Like many of its contemporaries, this 1962 Bristol MW6G would later be converted for OMO, being painted poppy red and fitted with bus seats during 1976, just months before withdrawal. *Photobus*

New in April 1962, LS808 (3808 PW), a Bristol MW6G with 39-seat coach bodywork, is pictured in June 1964 at Great Yarmouth, showing to advantage the Metropolitan fleetname which, in common with other Yarmouth-based coaches, it would retain until the end of the 1967 season. This vehicle would later be fitted for OMO and repainted red during 1976 but survived for just a further year before being taken out of service.
Maurice Doggett

Later versions of the new ECW coach body featured deeper, flush windscreens, as seen on Bristol MW6G LS831 (APW 831B) at Victoria Coach Station in December 1965. New in May 1964, being one of the first ECOC vehicles to feature a year-suffix registration, this coach would be withdrawn in 1980.
John Hypher

In 1964 ECW redesigned the front end of its MW coach body by deepening the windscreen and making it fit flush with the bodywork around it. New in 1964, LS826 (APW 826B) was among the last of this type to be purchased by ECOC before the company standardised on the rear-engined RELH for its heavyweight coaches. Seen loading at Cambridge bus station *en route* to Felixstowe during June 1972, it would remain in service until 1980. *Mark Hughes*

Bristol RELH6G coach RE892 (HAH 892D), with 47-seat ECW bodywork, makes a fine sight in its simple but attractive cream and maroon livery. New in March 1966, it would later receive NBC white livery, surviving thus until 1979. *Photobus*

Seen loading passengers in Cambridge prior to departing for Haverhill, Bristol RESL6G RS657 (KVF 657E), with 46-seat ECW bodywork, entered service in June 1967 and would remain in the fleet until 1981. *Photobus*

ECOC's first Bristol RELL6Gs, with ECW 53-seat bodywork, entered service during 1968. RL682 (RAH 682F) is seen at Crowland when brand-new before making the return journey to Peterborough. This fine vehicle would end its days as a source of spares for others of its type, ultimately being disposed of in July 1984. *John Hypher*

A departure from Bristol/ECW coaches came during 1967 with the purchase of four of these Bedford VAM14s with 45-seat Duple bodywork. Pictured in cream and maroon livery, CB837 (LNG 837E) would remain in the fleet until 1976. *R. H. G. Simpson*

New in May 1967 was this 45-seat Duple-bodied Bedford VAM14, CB837 (LNG 837E). Forsaking its stylish maroon and cream colour scheme for National white in 1972, it would remain with ECOC until 1976. *Photobus*

Looking splendid in Tilling livery is Peterborough-based FLF461 (KAH 461D) on its way out to Woodston during August 1973. Note, however, that the upper-deck cream band has been discontinued. This 1966 bus would go on to serve with ECOC for a further 11 years. *Malcolm Keeley*

61

Pictured at Lowestoft in August 1969 is SB662 (NAH 662F), a Bedford VAM5 with 41-seat ECW body. New in November 1967, it was to enjoy a relatively short life with the company, being withdrawn in 1976. *Maurice Doggett*

The first Bristol LH6Ps, with 45-seat ECW bodywork, were delivered in June 1968. Seen while still new at Peterborough bus station, LH686 (RAH 686F) would remain with the company for 12 years. *John Hypher*

relatively modern LS vehicles were adapted for stage-carriage use; many were fitted with bus-type destination indicators and bus seats and given red livery, while more modern vehicles were given jack-knife doors and fitted with OMO equipment. Six of the Bedford SBOs were also relegated to bus work and repainted red.

In order to extend its programme of OMO services, the company acquired 13 Bristol LS saloons from Eastern National in 1966, primarily for Norwich city services. A further 15 second-hand LS buses and coaches were also acquired from fellow Tilling-group operators during 1968 and, where appropriate, were modified for their service duties with the company, being fitted with OMO equipment and electrically powered doors. A pair of Bristol KSW open-toppers were also acquired from neighbouring Eastern National to replace the former Brighton, Hove & District Ks on the Felixstowe seafront service.

◄ New in 1954 as a cream-liveried coach, Bedford SBO BVS850 (PPW 850) picks up in Newmarket during July 1960. Relegated to bus work the previous year, being adapted for OMO, fitted with an electrically operated sliding door and repainted red, it nevertheless retained its coach seats, albeit reduced in number by two, to 35. This vehicle would remain in service until 1966. *Maurice Doggett*

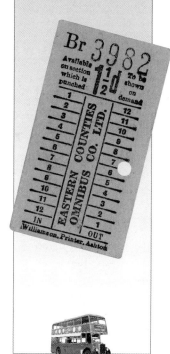

The effects of the social, economic and technological changes since the war had a knock-on effect on the number of passengers being carried by the company. There were no sudden changes, but as the 1950s progressed fewer people were going out for entertainment, preferring to stay at home and watch television, which was becoming more widely available (particularly on rental), while other journeys previously made by bus were increasingly being made by car, as this instantly accessible form of door-to-door travel became available to greater numbers of the population. By the early 1960s people's travel habits had changed beyond recognition, but ECOC continued to maintain the network through cross-subsidisation.

With falling revenue and rising costs the answer partly lay in expanding one-man operation, which was introduced gradually from the mid-1950s — a notable landmark, in December 1955, being the first OMO journey worked by a full-size bus (a Bristol SC on the 309 Dogsthorpe–Peterborough service) — and gained momentum through the 1960s. Vehicles suitable for this work had been purchased in significant numbers during this time in the shape of Bristol SCs, LSs, MWs and REs, OMO equipment being fitted as they were allocated to OMO duties.

The company had dozens of outstations across its territory, and a significant number of these ran OMO vehicles, making their operation more economic.

During the Tilling years nothing stood still. New services were introduced in all areas, others were curtailed or withdrawn, and numerous changes and amendments were put into place to keep abreast with local development and demand. All areas saw a rationalisation of services, which included renumbering into more logical geographic groupings. One major area of growth in many towns was the provision of new, extended and re-routed services to serve the new housing areas which were springing up. Services worthy of mention are the Lowestoft local route to the Whitton Estate, which started in 1956, and the introduction of local services in the expanding King's Lynn area throughout the 1950s and '60s. North Walsham also gained importance during the early 1950s as the focal point for a number of services in the area, while 1952 also saw the introduction of an early rail-replacement service between Wells and Heacham via Docking. Norwich city services also saw some revisions during the 1960s to cater for growth in the city area and the needs of university students.

►

Further open-top buses joined the fleet in January 1968 from neighbouring Eastern National, replacing the ex-BH&D vehicles. One of two 1953 Bristol KSW5Gs with ECW bodywork, LKO239 (WNO 482), photographed at Cromer bus station in August 1969, would continue in service for another couple of seasons, surviving until 1971.
Maurice Doggett

makers, British Railways started a programme of line closures. The Midland & Great Northern line, among others in Norfolk, was closed, and replacement bus services were introduced, many run by ECOC. The first of these started in March 1959 with services 401/2 running between King's Lynn and Great Yarmouth, and other routes continued to be added during the Beeching years. Many of these ran throughout Norfolk, but others also ran into Cambridge and Peterborough. All were numbered in the 4xx series, and, generally speaking, the passenger numbers carried were very low.

Of added interest in the Norwich District was the introduction in 1964 of the seasonal open-top service between Cromer and Sheringham, giving the company a second seafront service.

New services in the Ipswich District came with the purchase in 1951 of Beeston's of East Bergholt and of V. T. & J. Faiers (Clarke's Coaches) of Felixstowe, these acquisitions bringing respectively services to Colchester and local town routes in Felixstowe. Indeed, from May 1952 one of the ex-Faiers routes ran as an open-top Felixstowe seafront service each summer.

Cambridge District services saw a mixture of new routes and withdrawals in both the Ely and the Haverhill areas. New housing estates were also served in Newmarket, and in Cambridge a new service between Trumpington and Newmarket Road started in 1949. The early 1950s saw new local services starting in Peterborough, March and Wisbech to cater for new development in these towns; this development has continued, and Peterborough, in particular, has seen phenomenal and sustained growth which continues even to this day.

In the late 1950s, with the realisation, even prior to Beeching, that many of its rural rail services were heavy loss-

The 1960s witnessed the inauguration of new express services, many operated jointly with other operators to such destinations as Llandudno, Leicester and Hereford. In 1961 ECOC became a partner in the Associated Motorways network based on Cheltenham, with services running from Great Yarmouth, Norwich, Cambridge, Peterborough, Felixstowe and Ipswich, and from 1968 the company would become a partner in a pooling and operating agreement with Eastern National and Grey-Green to inter-work and market their express services throughout East Anglia under the East Anglian Express banner.

Under the terms of the Transport Act 1962 the BTC was abolished, the Transport Holding Co being created in its place to own and direct the Government's bus and other road activities, but again there were no outward differences to ECOC or its operations. This all changed, however, under the 1968 Transport Act, which among other things created the National Bus Company (NBC) from 1 January 1969. All of ECOC's assets were vested in the new company, and the effects of NBC ownership will be described in the next chapter.

5. Part of the National Bus Company

The newly created National Bus Company (NBC) brought together the already nationalised Tilling Group and the UK passenger transport division of British Electric Traction. BET bus companies were already partly owned by the state through its shareholdings via the railway companies from the late 1920s, and the Government purchased the remaining equity in these concerns. Indeed, NBC brought together again many companies which had previously (prior to the break-up of TBAT in 1942) been associated. One could be forgiven during the early days of NBC for believing that things would continue much the same for ECOC as during the Tilling days. Behind the scenes, however, a group corporate identity was being formulated, and a new organisational, regional and headquarters structure was being put into place.

Between 1969 and 1971 more Bristol RELL and LH buses were purchased, together with some dual-purpose RELLs. ECOC had a brief flirtation with the then fashionable dual-entrance/exit layout, but all seven RELLs so equipped would be rebuilt to front-entrance configuration during 1972. Further RELH coaches were delivered, but interestingly the three 1971 vehicles were fitted with 49-seat coachwork by Plaxton, the first of this make to be ordered by the company.

The highlight of 1969 was the arrival of the fleet's first rear-engined double-deckers. Designated as the VRT, this front-entrance, 70-seat Bristol/ECW design superseded the front-engined Lodekka and fitted in with the Government's desire to implement more one-man operation throughout the UK. Indeed, A clause of the 1968 Transport Act made available to operators a grant of 25% towards the cost of new vehicles of approved designs to modernise their fleets and extend OMO — for the operators it was an attractive offer of 'Buy four new buses and get one free!' Three of ECOC's 1970 VRTs were delivered in an attractive experimental OMO livery for double-deckers consisting of cream window surrounds and a wide cream band between decks, but within a few months they would be repainted into standard colours. Apart from its large intake of new vehicles, ECOC was continuing to receive surplus vehicles from former Tilling companies, to maintain its OMO

programme. As before, these were Bristol LS saloons and, where appropriate, were fitted for OMO by the company.

Another demonstrator to add to the list of those operated was the prototype ECW-bodied Bristol LH, which, having done the rounds of various operators during the previous couple of years, was purchased from Bristol Commercial Vehicles in 1970. In the same year ECOC also acquired five short-length Bristol LHS buses from Luton Corporation, which had sold its bus operation to United Counties; excluded from the sale, they were brand-new, not having been operated by Luton prior to the takeover, and were re-registered before entering service with ECOC.

Service revisions continued under the new regime. The first, in 1969, affected Costessey services, and this presaged wider changes in July 1971, whereby the Norwich city network was completely revamped and renumbered into a new 500 series; at the same time the forecourt of Norwich Thorpe station was abandoned as a terminus for the company's services, and the nearby head office in Thorpe Road was extended to accommodate more staff. In June 1971 Ipswich services had also undergone a complete revision and renumbering, and at the end of the season all open-top services were abandoned, prompting the withdrawal of the ex-Eastern National Bristol KSWs.

The years 1972-5 were eventful for ECOC in terms of vehicles, services and the emergence of NBC's stamp of ownership. The last new Bristol RELL buses entered service during 1972, but the number of VRTs continued to grow steadily, as did their areas of operation. Bristol LH saloon LH537 was exhibited at the Commercial Motor Show that year and was the first ECOC vehicle to be delivered in the new corporate poppy red, one of the two main alternative colours for NBC fleets. The first poppy-red double-deckers were VR399-401, which arrived in November 1972 complete with white waistband, white block-capital fleetnames with 'double N' logos and grey wheels. The first coaches to arrive in the new all-white National livery were a trio of Plaxton-bodied Bristol RELHs, which joined the fleet in June 1973.

An ECW-bodied Bristol LS5G, LE755 (OAH 755) started life in April 1954 as a cream-and-maroon-liveried coach, numbered LS755; it was converted for OMO and fitted with bus-type destination display during 1963 and repainted into this pleasing livery in 1970. Captured on film operating on the 336 service between King's Lynn and Peterborough, it would remain in service until 1972. *Photobus*

Until the arrival of the Leyland National the Bristol RELL6G was the standard large-capacity single-decker. An early example, its 53-seat ECW body featuring a flat windscreen, was RL704 (TVF 704G), which entered service in May 1969. Seen in Cambridge during June 1972, it was to remain in service until 1984. *Mark Hughes*

Dual-purpose RLE866 (WPW 866H) was delivered in April 1970 in this attractive coach livery. An RELL6G with semi-coach seats for 50 passengers, it would be repainted in Tilling red and cream during 1971 and then poppy red and white a couple of years later. This vehicle would have a short working life of just eight years, being withdrawn in 1978. *Photobus*

Representing the many Bristol LS saloons acquired to extend the company's OMO programme is LM847 (XNU 418), a 1955 LS6G which came from Midland General in March 1969. Despite being fitted with semi-coach seats, for 43 passengers, it is seen taking up duty on Norwich city service 90A to Cringleford, in August 1969. Its working life with ECOC would end in 1971 following the delivery of new vehicles. *Maurice Doggett*

Representing the shorter version of the standard LH model and seating 37 within its ECW body, LHS598 was one of five Bristol LHS6P buses acquired unused from Luton Corporation Transport in February 1970. It is seen in Peterborough bus station in August 1976, preparing to depart for Walton. Renumbered as LHS935 in 1977, it would be withdrawn three years later.
Mark Hughes

A Bristol LH6P with 45-seat ECW bodywork to the revised style with curved windscreen, LH535 (GNG 535K) was photographed in Cambridge during September 1979. New in 1972, it was to spend only eight years in service before being discarded.
Malcolm Keeley

Just three months old when photographed leaving Cambridge bus station for Peterborough in June 1972, VR396 (ENG 396K) was among the last Bristol VRTs to be delivered in Tilling red and cream. It would later be adorned in the overall-white livery of the London & Manchester Assurance Society, before succumbing to the inevitable poppy red.
Mark Hughes

More of the same were delivered the following year, as were four Bedford YRTs with 53-seat Duple bodywork. With the takeover of the Norwich operations of Mascot Coaches (described later in this chapter) a couple of the Bedfords carried Mascot National fleetnames, while the REs were equipped for OMO to qualify for Bus Grant. The company's last new REs, delivered during the latter part of 1974, were eight dual-purpose RELH vehicles which were unusual in combining bus-style bodywork with all-white National coach livery.

Most single-deck deliveries consisted of Leyland Nationals, of which the first two arrived at the end of 1972. These, together with other Nationals arriving over the next couple of years, were painted in all-over poppy red but later received white relief, which considerably enhanced their appearance. Built by the Leyland National Co Ltd — a joint venture between Leyland Vehicles and the National Bus Company — at a new plant near Workington, Cumbria, the type was to become ubiquitous not merely with ECOC but throughout NBC and elsewhere.

Following a catalogue of problems and failures the Scottish Bus Group (SBG) had completely lost faith in its VRTs and decided to rid itself of these buses, and NBC, keen to extend one-man operation, agreed to an exchange involving some of its newest FLFs on a one-for-one basis. During 1973, in exchange for 46 of its latest Bristol FLFs, ECOC received 30 Bristol VRTs (of which 12 were of the longer VRTLL variety, seating 83); the company should have received 46 VRTs, but the balance went instead to Lincolnshire Road Car (10) and Eastern National (6), which neighbouring NBC subsidiaries passed to ECOC equivalent numbers of older FLFs, together with a few older LDs. As with other VRTs in the ECOC fleet, the ex-SBG vehicles were equipped for OMO. Of the FLFs, seven of those acquired from Lincolnshire and all six from Eastern National were fitted with Cave-Brown-Cave heating, tripling the number of such buses in the ECOC fleet.

Cheltenham coach station provides the backdrop for RE850 (SAH 850M) during August 1977. A Bristol RELH6G with 49-seat Plaxton coachwork, this vehicle was new in June 1974, being fitted for OMO five months later. It would pass to Ambassador in 1984 when ECOC was split into three separate companies. *Mark Hughes*

Between 1972 and 1974 a number of buses of various types were painted into an experimental livery of dark red and white. However, this was short-lived, and at their next repaint the vehicles in question were painted poppy red, as indeed was the rest of the bus fleet. Coaches were repainted in National white from 1972.

Overall advertisement liveries made their debut in the fleet in 1972, and over the following years FLFs, RELLs, VRTs and Leyland Nationals received some colourful and attractive schemes. One of the earliest, applied in May 1972 to promote the company's own parcels service, saw RL735 painted overall brown and signwritten to resemble a parcel, which scheme this bus continued to wear (albeit with price alterations etc) until September 1984 — a UK record for a continuous overall advertisement on a bus. Another notable livery was that applied at the end of 1976 to VR144, which was painted silver with blue relief to celebrate HM the Queen's Silver Jubilee the following year and ran thus throughout 1977 before reverting to poppy red.

▲ New to ECOC in February 1974, CB847 (PPW 847M), a Bedford YRT with 53-seat Duple coachwork, received its Mascot National fleetnames the following month. Caught on film at Hunstanton in June 1974, it was to enjoy a very short stay with the company, being transferred to National Travel (South East) in February 1975. *Maurice Doggett*

◄ The eight dual-purpose Bristol RELH6L/ECW 49-seaters of 1974 were unusual for ECOC in employing bus (rather than coach) bodyshells but were nevertheless given National white coach livery. Despite this and its relative luxury, RLE743 (GCL 345N), new in October 1974, was working a Norwich city service when photographed during the summer of 1975. In common with the rest of the batch it would have its Leyland 680 engine replaced by a Gardner 6HLX unit, in 1981, and would pass to Cambus in September 1984. *John Hypher*

The Leyland National became the standard large-capacity single-decker in the majority of NBC fleets. Among the first to join ECOC was 52-seat LN542 (HVF 542L), which arrived in February 1973 and is seen on Norwich city service 525 to Drayton during the summer of 1975.
John Hypher

Photographed outside Cremorne Lane Works during February 1976, VR302 (LFS 304F) had just received a repaint and had a standard two-piece route/destination display fitted in place of its SBG-style trapezoid original. Seating 83 passengers, being some 2ft 4in longer than the more common VRTSL, this Bristol VRTLL6G was acquired in February 1973 as part of the SBG/NBC Bristol FLF/VRT exchanges. New to Scottish Omnibuses in December 1968, it would be withdrawn by ECOC in 1980.
John Hypher

Bristol MW5G LS794 (7794 NG) in NBC dual-purpose livery at Ipswich during February 1975, just a year before its withdrawal. New in 1960 as a front-line coach, it was fitted with these bus-type destination indicators in 1965 but not relegated to bus duties until 1969. OMO conversion was carried out by ECW in January 1971.
Maurice Doggett

ECOC had six of these 30ft Bristol FL6B Lodekkas. Delivered in 1963 with open platforms, they later received platform doors, LFL59 (559 BPW) being so fitted in 1972, in which year it also had its Bristol BVW engine replaced by a Gardner 6LW unit. Seen on Norwich city service 502 during August 1980, it would be withdrawn the following year.
Malcolm Keeley

Seen at Cromer bus station during the summer of 1976 before leaving for London on National Express service 092 is LS806 (3806 PW), in the National white livery applied during 1972. This MW6G, new in 1962, was another to be converted and repainted for bus duties in 1976 yet withdrawn before the year was out.
John Hypher

A view of Bristol MW6G LS819 (819 BNG) at Peterborough bus station, showing this former coach after downgrading to bus duties. In June 1975 it was converted for OMO, fitted with bus seats and bus-type destination display and repainted in poppy red by Marshall's of Cambridge, continuing thus until withdrawal in 1978.
Mark Hughes

Photographed just before withdrawal in 1974 was CB841 (PPW 841F), a Bedford VAM70 with 45-seat Duple coachwork. This coach had entered service in May 1968 in maroon and cream and gained National white livery during 1973. *Mark Hughes*

A Bristol RELH6G with 47-seat ECW coachwork, RE898 (SVF 898G) is seen at Peterborough bus station in August 1976. Delivered in February 1969 in cream and maroon, it was painted National white during 1973 and would be withdrawn from service in 1980. *Mark Hughes*

More major revisions took place during March 1972, this time to Peterborough city services, the routes being renumbered into a new series starting at 380. In Norwich a Christmas park-and-ride service between Heigham Street and City Hall was run in conjunction with the City Council in December 1972, and a revised route was operated the following spring. The original route was repeated the following Christmas and subsequently until 1976, when the service ran every Saturday.

In January 1973 it was the turn of services in northeast Suffolk to be revamped, these being renumbered into the 7xx series, and the following month, still in Suffolk, town services in Bury St Edmunds were revised and renumbered into the 9xx series. Cambridge city services were similarly treated in April, being renumbered in a new series starting at 180. Between May and August an orange-liveried 19-seat Morrison Electrocar battery-driven bus was operated on loan from the Department of Trade & Industry, to assess the suitability of battery-electric power (as an alternative to diesel) on all-day town and city services. Until July it was used on a half-hourly service between Norwich Thorpe station and the Norfolk & Norwich Hospital;

during August it ran in Peterborough on a circular route of the city. Yet more revisions were implemented by ECOC in October, these focusing on West Suffolk and Thetford, new service numbers being allocated in the 9xx and 99x series respectively.

During 1973 all NBC express-coach services were placed under the control of the Central Activities Group. NBC's coach territory was divided into five National Travel areas, ECOC falling within the remit of National Travel (South East). Renumbered into an 0xx series, East Anglian services (always marketed as simply 'Anglian'), were removed from ECOC control but contracted back under a system whereby the company was paid to provide the coaches and run the service for National Travel.

During 1973/4 ECOC was suffering from an acute shortage of serviceable vehicles, the main problem being the non-availability of spare parts. The practice of robbing Peter to pay Paul had run its course, and huge numbers of vehicles now awaited repair without the necessary parts' being available. Other vehicles which would normally have been brought in

EASTERN COUNTIES

◄ Pictured at Ipswich's Old Cattle Market bus station in August 1974 is Bristol FLF6G FLF458 (JPW 458D), adorned as a mobile advertisement for the London & Manchester Assurance Society. It carried this livery from March 1973 to September 1975 and was withdrawn during 1984. *Malcolm Gee*

for minor attention had to keep running (safely, it should be added), but the vehicle examiners took a different view and took dozens more buses off the road for seemingly trivial reasons. As a consequence ECOC hired in dozens of vehicles to maintain services, and at times it looked as if a co-operative of East Anglian operators had taken over! Things eventually got back to normal, and by the end of 1974 the face of ECOC was once again seen throughout the region.

Meanwhile the Traffic Department was busy with yet another raft of major service revisions and renumberings, effected in March 1974. These involved West Norfolk, where services took numbers in the 3xx and 4xx series, Great Yarmouth and Lowestoft, which adopted the 6xx series, and a new series of town services operated jointly with Lowestoft Corporation (from April renamed Waveney UDC), numbered from 680 upwards.

March 1974 was a busy month for the company, for it also saw the takeover, jointly with National Travel (South East), of the Norwich branch of Mascot Coaches, the new unit being named Mascot National. ECOC's share of the spoils

A familiar sight for many years was this Bristol RELL6G, RL735 (AAH 735J), in its brown parcel livery, being seen thus at Ipswich in July 1974. Delivered in 1971, it received its brown paintwork in September 1972 and continued in this guise until September 1984, when it finally succumbed to the poppy-red paintbrush; as such it holds the record for the longest-running overall advertisement in the UK. Upon release from the paintshops it was, ironically, transferred to Cambus.
Maurice Doggett

Bristol Lodekka FS5G towing wagon X59 (49 CNG) was formerly bus LFS49, with open-platform double-deck bodywork. Converted in February 1975, it is seen in Surrey Street bus station, Norwich, soon after being outshopped. *John Hypher*

Photographed during the winter of 1975/6, Norwich-based AEC Matador breakdown wagon X38 rescues Bristol FS LFS76 (AAH 614B) by means of a rigid tow. Affectionately known as 'Jumbo' by the engineering staff, it was converted for this purpose during 1961 and would be retained until 1978.
John Hypher

A Bristol Lodekka FS5G new in 1965, LFS125 (GNG 125C) became part of the driver-training fleet during August 1976. Renumbered X66, it was photographed at Surrey Street bus station, Norwich, soon after conversion and repaint into yellow livery.
John Hypher

79

A 52-seat Leyland National which joined the fleet in September 1977, LN586 (WAH 586S) is seen here as a typical NBC bus but in 1982 was repainted into a livery of white with a broad red band. It would remain with Eastern Counties after privatisation.
Maurice Doggett

▲ consisted of a couple of Bedford YRQ coaches, a travel office in Castle Meadow, some excursion licences and a service to the University.

The last in the programme of major service revisions, this time affecting South Norfolk, took effect from May 1975, routes taking new numbers in the 8xx series. The year turned out to be one of new special services, these starting in October with the Ipswich 'Get You Home' service. This ran on weekday evenings from the north of the town to bring people into Ipswich for entertainment by 19.30, returning at 21.20 and 22.15 and setting down as required along selected roads. Perhaps the most significant innovation, however, was the first Norfolk community minibus scheme, which took to the roads in November. Operated by a Ford Transit minibus supplied by the company but manned by local volunteer drivers, it provided a service between six tiny villages and Holt or Fakenham, where there were connections with other ECOC services; further villages would be added in 1977. The scheme was run in partnership with Norfolk County Council, which financed the operation, services running to a timetable drawn up by the village bus committee. The bus itself was painted poppy red with a vertical wrap-around white band and 'National Norfolk' fleetname.

Finally, a Christmas park-and-ride service was operated in Cambridge from the Cattle Market to Emmanuel Street between October 1975 and January 1976 and ran again from November 1976; by 1981 this service would be running every Saturday throughout the year as well as on weekdays in the run-up to Christmas.

Turning to events during the second half of the decade, a healthy influx of new vehicles continued to arrive. All new double-deck deliveries were of the Bristol VRT, now in Series 3 form and with bodywork to a revised style featuring curved windscreens; of these VR172, a 1976 vehicle, was the 2,500th vehicle (new or second-hand) to enter service with the company and received a commemorative plaque. Leyland Nationals made up the vast majority of new single-deckers, although a further 15 Bristol LHs arrived in 1977/8. A 25-seat Ford A0609 entered service in 1976 at Huntingdon (of which more anon), and a pair of 12-seat Ford Transits arrived during 1978 for the village community schemes. Another Transit was purchased from Norfolk County Council in 1979 but had to be brought up to full PSV specification before entering service.

Between 1976 and 1979 the company took delivery of 31 new coaches, all 49-seat Leyland Leopards, with a mix of Alexander, Duple, Willowbrook and Plaxton bodywork. Some were equipped for OMO and accrued mileage on such work to fulfil obligations relating to Bus Grant. Second-hand purchases, in 1978 from National Travel (South East), comprised six Bristol RELHs, four with Plaxton bodywork and two ECW. The following year more cast-offs arrived in the shape of Leopards from National Travel (London) and Ribble; the former were 12m long, the first vehicles of this length in the fleet.

In January 1976 National Travel (South East) assumed full control of Mascot National but did not require the premises in Vulcan Road; these passed to ECOC and were redeveloped as a depot for Norwich city services, opening as such in August.

Joint services in Lowestoft ended in March 1976 after a couple of years, and following a prior Traffic Court hearing, at which both the local authority and ECOC had applied for all the town service licences, the company was granted all save one,

Typical of the Ford Transits in use on the various Norfolk County Council community-bus schemes was MB996 (DCL 996T). New in November 1978, it had a 12-seat Tricentrol body and is shown here with an incorrect MD prefix to its fleet number. This bus would be taken out of service during 1984. *R. H. G. Simpson*

A Leyland Leopard PSU3C/4R with 49-seat Alexander body, LL752 (MCL 934P) entered service in May 1976. It is seen on park-and-ride work in Cambridge in May 1977, still in the dual-purpose livery it wore when new. *Maurice Doggett*

In the late 1970s ECOC ordered Leopards with various makes of coachwork. Representing Plaxton is 49-seat LP816 (JVF 816V), which entered service in February 1980. Seen in Cambridge in June 1983 on National Express service 098 to London, this coach would pass to Ambassador Travel upon the division of ECOC in 1984. *Maurice Doggett*

Photographed in Birmingham *en route* to Leicester during April 1984 is Leyland Leopard LL812 (JCL 812V) with 49-seat Willowbrook coachwork. Fitted for OMO from new, this coach was painted in National white livery when delivered in November 1979, receiving these colours in November 1982. In September 1984 it would be transferred to Ambassador Travel. *Malcolm Keeley*

Leyland Leopard LL803 (HVG 803V), with 49-seat Duple body, at Reading bus station a month after entering service, in March 1980. It would pass to Ambassador in September 1984. *Mark Hughes*

between Pakefield and Gunton Estate; this was run by Waveney UDC until December 1977, when the municipal undertaking ceased operating buses altogether and the service passed to ECOC.

During May 1976 an experimental midibus service was started in Huntingdon and St Ives, using the aforementioned 25-seat Ford midibus. This featured peak-hour, shopping and dial-a-ride services to and from villages in the area and included the Yaxley 'dial-a-bus', St Ives shopping services, a commuter service to/from Huntingdon station, an Alconbury–Huntingdon doorstep service, a Sawtry village service and Oundle market-day services. In August 1978 the Ford was replaced by a Bristol LHS with Cambridgeshire Pick-Me-Up branding on its sides. Subsequently a Bristol RELL and a VRT would be used, and services modified in the light of local requirements.

November 1976 saw the introduction of the Norwich 'Shopper Hopper'. Planned and funded by the City Council, this ran on a circular route around the city every 10 minutes but was poorly used. The Council revised and re-branded the service as 'Centrelink', reintroducing it at the end of January 1977; in this form it fared rather better, surviving until June 1979.

In June 1978 a second Norfolk community minibus was launched, serving villages in the North Walsham, Aldborough and Cromer areas, and in June 1980 this was followed by a third, based on Denton and Alburgh.

Heralding a return of seasonal open-top workings, between June and September 1978 an open-top Bristol LDL was borrowed from Western National for the Felixstowe seafront service. The following year it was purchased, together with a similar sister vehicle, and for use on the Cromer–Sheringham service.

A notable acquisition in June 1979 was that of old-established and well-respected Cambridgeshire operator Burwell & District. Its services were integrated into the ECOC network but none of its vehicles was retained, all passing to a dealer the same month.

As the 1980s dawned further new Bristol VRT double-deckers joined the fleet together with four second-hand examples, which came from East Midland in 1983. The last new VRTs arrived in 1981, and one of these, VR294, was the last VRT to be bodied by Eastern Coach Works for NBC. Single-

deckers comprised the new Leyland National 2 and some more Ford Transits, which were joined by nine second-hand Bristol RELLs from Alder Valley. Coaches were again represented by the Leyland Leopard, with coachwork split between Duple and Willowbrook. Indeed, in 1982/3 coaches constituted the entire intake of new vehicles, although (as previously) some were fitted for OMO. The 1982 deliveries were further Leyland Leopards, this time with ECW bodywork, but the following year saw the first Plaxton-bodied Leyland Tigers enter the fleet.

With the long-standing bus-company practice of cross-subsidising services becoming impracticable due to falling passenger numbers, falling receipts and higher costs, the Local Government Acts of 1972 and 1974 had given county councils new powers and a statutory duty to develop policies to promote co-ordinated and efficient public-transport systems. They had to produce a comprehensive public-transport plan, and all the bus companies had a statutory obligation to co-operate with the county councils to achieve this. To this end the bus companies were required to advise the counties of those services/timings which they would operate commercially, and the counties had the powers and funding to buy in such services/timings as they

▲ Purchased for experimental community services in the Huntingdon and St Ives areas, which started during May 1976, was this Ford A0609 midibus with 25-seat Alexander (Belfast) body. It was photographed when brand-new outside Cremorne Lane Works in Norwich in April 1976 before entering service. Replaced by a Bristol LHS, it would be withdrawn in 1979, becoming company publicity vehicle X78 in September 1980 before being sold the following year.
Maurice Doggett

Purchased second-hand from East Midland in July 1983, Bristol VRT/ECW VR408 (HAL 104K) gleams in the Cambridge sunshine a year later, during July 1984. New to its previous owner in 1971, it would become part of the Cambus fleet in September 1984. *Malcolm Keeley*

For the 1978 summer season this open-top Bristol LDL6G was received on loan from Western National to operate the Felixstowe seafront service. Carrying temporary fleet number F1, it ran in the proper fleet colours of red and white livery thanks to previous use by Devon General; it was acquired, together with a similar bus, in June 1979. New in December 1957, OT2 (VDV 753) was to remain in service until 1987. Still looking good after 23 years, it was photographed at Felixstowe during August 1980. *Malcolm Keeley*

Delivered during November 1980 in all-over poppy red was Leyland National 2 LN610 (PEX 610W), with seating for 49 passengers. Seen in Surrey Street bus station, Norwich, it would remain with ECOC following the 1984 company split. *R. H. G. Simpson*

Seen at Showbus at Woburn Abbey in September 1982, LN624 (UVF 624X), a 49-seat Leyland National 2, was new in October 1981 painted in 'red stripe' livery.
Mark Hughes

Duple-bodied Leyland Leopard PSU3F/4R coach LL824 (RNG 824W) was new to the company in April 1981 and is pictured between express duties at Victoria Coach Station in November 1982. It would be transferred to Ambassador Travel in September 1984, when ECOC's coaching operation passed to this newly formed company. *Maurice Doggett*

saw fit. Sometimes these would be contracted to the main operator (e.g. ECOC) or, indeed, to any other operator chosen by the county having due regard to costs, reliability etc. More changes took place to ECOC's services during the NBC days than at any other time in its history, and more were to follow. During 1979, in common with other subsidiaries, it carried out detailed company-wide surveys as part of an NBC initiative known as Market Analysis Project (MAP), which was designed to tailor routes and timings around data received. The resultant services provided a completely new commercial network and gave the company much-needed savings by shedding loss-making services and infrastructure. The county councils were consulted in the design of the new networks and were able to use the data to identify areas outside the network which they considered socially necessary and which might require funding. During the 1980s services throughout the company's area were completely revised, and many long-established but loss-making routes were removed from the timetable. Indeed, ECOC withdrew from whole swathes of territory, opening the door for independent operators to fill the gaps and create their own new networks.

The early 1980s witnessed the introduction of numerous branded coach services. From the autumn of 1980 fast journeys between Norwich and London were branded 'Norfolk Flyer', setting the style for other coach services to/from London; the 'West Norfolk Flyer' from King's Lynn started in April 1981 and the 'Mid Norfolk Flyer' from Wells in May, the 'Fenland Flyer' from Hunstanton being added a couple of years later. Meanwhile, in December 1980, the 'Hereward Harrier' express service was introduced as an extra link between Peterborough and London taking in the Orton Townships, its success leading to a greatly increased service from March 1982. In April 1981 two new services started between Cambridge and London, operated jointly with Green Line, ECOC using Leyland Leopards in a new livery of white with a broad red waistband and large white fleetnames. A further service was added in June 1982, following a third route into London.

In March 1982 the new Queensgate bus station opened in Peterborough, and in June the Peterborough–Spalding service was extended to Boston and Skegness, becoming jointly operated with Lincolnshire Road Car. A new series of limited-

stop services, branded as Eastline, started running from June, further routes being introduced at intervals until July 1984. These featured Leyland Leopard coaches in white livery with the broad red band and large fleetnames. Services linked Cambridge with Great Yarmouth, Bury St Edmunds with Norwich, Ipswich with Cambridge, Overstrand with Peterborough and Norwich with Peterborough. From March 1982 a further Leopard, in BR blue and grey, ran for a year on a rail-link service between King's Lynn and Peterborough. On the bus front, a fourth Norfolk Community Minibus scheme, based on Docking, was established in November.

Part of the White Paper 'Buses', published in 1984, outlined the Government's intention to reorganise NBC into smaller free-standing units ready for transfer to the private sector, although a start had already been made on this process prior to publication, some subsidiaries having already been split into smaller units. On 9 September 1984 the surgeon's knife cut into ECOC, the western area being separated from the main company and renamed Cambus Ltd. This was a stand-alone company within

▲ Purchased as a replacement for an earlier Tricentrol-bodied Transit, this Mellor-bodied 16-seater Ford Transit was delivered in 1984 for use as the Sharrington community bus. Its more bus-like design gave passengers easier access than did previous minibuses. Photographed at Sharrington in August 1986, MB991 (A991 LVG) would be transferred to Norfolk County Council at the end of 1987.
Maurice Doggett

NBC, with its own management team led by Managing Director Paul Merryweather, and adopted pale blue and white as its basic fleet livery. Similarly, the coaching arm of ECOC became Ambassador Travel (Eastern Counties) Ltd, again as a stand-alone company, under Managing Director John Madgett. The remaining eastern area continued to operate as a much smaller ECOC, covering Norfolk and Suffolk under Managing Director Peter Brundle. Eighty-three coaches passed to Ambassador and 174 vehicles to Cambus, the balance of 259 remaining with ECOC.

Vehicles joining the ECOC fleet in 1984 consisted of a pair of Plaxton-bodied Leyland Tigers, three Ford Transits, a trio of ex-City of Oxford Bristol VRTs and three nearly new MCW Metroliner double-deck coaches from Midland Red (Express), exchanged for a similar number of recent Plaxton-bodied Tigers.

In 1985 ECOC began to feel the effects of the minibus mania which was sweeping NBC. The first influx comprised 36 Transits with a mix of Carlyle and Dormobile 16-seat converted van bodies (and a single Mellor-bodied example as a community-scheme replacement vehicle). These were used from October 1985 on a new series of high-frequency Norwich city services and carried Cityline branding; from the same month minibuses also ran on a new service between Sheringham, Cromer and Overstrand. The following year 105 new minibuses entered service on town routes at Felixstowe (April), King's Lynn (May), Bury St Edmunds (May), Lowestoft (July) — the latter from a new depot — and, throughout the year, in Norwich. These new vehicles consisted of 40 Freight Rovers, 35 Mercedes-Benz and a further 30 Transits, with van bodies converted by Dormobile, Alexander and Robin Hood.

Cambus chose a livery of pale blue and white. Now numbered 213, the one-time ECOC LN564 (PVF 364R) lays the usual Leyland National smokescreen as it departs Cambridge bus station for Earith in May 1985. *Mark Hughes*

Pictured between duties at Cambridge bus station during May 1985 is Leyland Leopard LL878 (CAH 878Y), with 47-seat ECW bodywork. New in August 1982, this coach was delivered in National Holidays livery and transferred to Ambassador Travel in September 1984. *Mark Hughes*

Recorded soon after privatisation, this view shows minibus MB754 (C754 BEX) at Norwich Thorpe station in overall blue advertising livery for Barclays Bank. New in May 1986, this vehicle is a Mercedes-Benz L608D with 20-seat bodywork conversion by Robin Hood. *Malcolm Gee*

Minibuses operating outside Norwich carried Miniline branding. Some of these vehicles also featured overall advertisements, in the same manner as their larger counterparts. The large-scale introduction of minibus operation in 1985/6 coincided with the renumbering of many ECOC routes into single or double figures.

Among all the new minibuses, four ex-Hastings & District full-height (14ft 6in) Bristol VRTs entered service on Norwich city services in 1985 and were recognisable through having yellow waistbands and roofs. The same year saw the acquisition from Ribble of 14 standard-height (13ft 8in) VRTs, of which two were converted to open-top for seafront duties. Another open-top conversion was effected in May 1985, when VR152 lost its roof and was repainted in 'venetian blind' livery of white with yellow, red and black horizontal stripes; a similar scheme had been applied the previous year to some VRTs that had been re-fitted with coach seats for long-distance limited-stop services. Further second-hand vehicles were acquired from West Riding, in the shape of four Leyland Leopard coaches with Alexander bodywork.

During 1986 open-toppers operated on summer Sundays at Hunstanton, although this would not be repeated in subsequent years. A number of VRTs were painted into a new livery of poppy red with a yellow waistband lined-out in black with a red line running through the yellow, but this was not pursued further.

Meanwhile, Ambassador Travel acquired three Leyland Tigers from Wessex National and a further example from North Devon during 1985. In addition to the MCW Metroliners transferred from ECOC, another joined the fleet during 1987 from Midland Red (North). Ambassador's operations comprised Eastline services from Peterborough to Felixstowe, worked jointly with Premier Travel of Cambridge, and, for a short while, a handful of journeys between Brandon and Cambridge; it also ran excursions and tours and National Express services from ECOC and Cambus depots. In December 1985, however, all express and excursion work in the Cambus operating area passed to that company, following which Ambassador's operations were confined largely to Norwich and Great Yarmouth, comprising excursions and tours from Yarmouth, the Norwich–London express service and UK and Continental holiday tours.

Between 1984 and 1986 Cambus purchased a quantity of second-hand vehicles, including 13 Bristol VRTs from various fellow NBC companies, 17 Leyland Nationals from Greater Manchester PTE, 24 Leyland Leopard and Tiger coaches from Ambassador and half a dozen Leopards from Cowie (better known as Grey-Green). Cambus too was caught up in the prevailing minibus mania, and 48 (Freight Rovers and Ford Transits) were purchased for revised city services in Cambridge and Peterborough. Operational changes continued under the new regime. During the summer of 1985 an open-top service using a Bristol FLF was operated from Peterborough to the nearby Nene Valley Railway, in August the depot in Cambridge was moved from the old Ortona building in Hills Road to a new site in Cowley Road, and in October the Saturday park-and-ride service in Cambridge was revised to run between Cowley Road and the Cattle Market via the city centre. The following year saw major changes to services in both cities. The second round of revisions in Peterborough took place in April, when four new Minishuttle services were inaugurated. The first Minishuttles in Cambridge started in June, and as part of major changes, further such routes were introduced in October, bringing the total to seven.

Part of the Transport Act 1985 dealt with the NBC disposal programme and required NBC to take such steps as might be practicable to ensure that its managers were afforded a reasonable opportunity of acquiring a controlling interest in the equity share capital of their companies. As far as the sale of ECOC, Cambus and Ambassador was concerned, this was indeed the case, and these companies were sold to their management teams. The first to be privatised was Cambus, which was sold by NBC on 5 December 1986. This was followed by the sales of ECOC on 26 February 1987 and of Ambassador Travel on 4 December 1987.

Thus our story draws to a close. Each of the companies has gone its own way, and their subsequent histories have followed very different paths. Even their names have now all but disappeared, but that of Eastern Counties will live on with those who travelled on its buses, with those who worked for the company and with those for whom the red buses were a familiar sight throughout their part of East Anglia.

With a couple of new minibuses in the background, VR383 (OCK 993K) pauses in Castle Meadow, Norwich, to pick up passengers during February 1987. This Series 2 Bristol VRT, dating from 1972, was purchased from Ribble in June 1985. *Richard Hunt*

Among the very last Bristol VRTs to be delivered, in November 1981, was VR284 (VEX 284X). New in poppy red, in June 1984 this bus was re-seated with coach seats for long-distance services, being repainted in 'red stripe' livery at the same time. Displaying the 'venetian blind' local-coach colours applied in January 1986, it is seen in November of that year, about to depart from Surrey Street bus station on Eastline service 794 to Peterborough. *Richard Hunt*

The new generation of open-topper is represented here by OT5 (OCK 995K), a Series 2 Bristol VRT, seen inside Great Yarmouth depot in September 1986. This was one of 14 such buses purchased from Ribble during 1985 and the second of a pair converted to open-top in 1986. It is painted in 'venetian blind' local-coach livery. *Richard Hunt*

Acknowledgements

I acknowledge with grateful thanks the following people and organisations for their valuable help in the preparation of this book: John Banks, Arnold Richardson of Photobus, Mark Hughes, Malcolm Keeley, Richard Hunt, Malcolm Gee, J. H. Aston, A. B. Cross, the Southdown Enthusiasts' Club and R. H. G. Simpson, for their superb photographs and transparencies and for their ready willingness for these to be reproduced in this volume, John Hutchinson of the Eastern Transport Collection Society, for providing me with useful contacts, and the Cambridgeshire Collection and Norwich Records Office, for information from their archives. My thanks are also extended to the PSV Circle, for kindly allowing me to draw information from their highly detailed Eastern Counties fleet history during the preparation of this book.

I am indebted to Bernard Simpson for his invaluable and ready expert help with timetables and for providing me with the detailed route and service information which I was seeking. My thanks also go to the late F. D. Simpson, for the use of his service-development charts.

Particular thanks go to Maurice Doggett, for putting at my disposal his vast collection of Eastern Counties photographs and for so willingly allowing me to make my selection for this book. Maurice also kindly checked the manuscript and photo captions, and I am grateful to him for his comments, corrections, advice and additional information, much of which has been incorporated into this book.

Last but by no means least, special thanks are due to my wife Lynda for her computer wizardry during the preparation of this volume and also for her forbearance in doing some of those domestic things that I should have been doing instead of enjoying myself writing about the glory days of Eastern Counties!

Gleaming like new, 1950-built Bristol LL5G/ECW LL718 (KNG 718) keeps alive the name and traditional livery of Eastern Counties at Showbus, Duxford, in September 2004. Now part of the Eastern Transport Collection, this bus was one of many similar vehicles which could once be seen throughout East Anglia. *John Hypher*